insight text guide

Victoria Bladen

Measure for Measure

William Shakespeare

insight™

▶ innovative ▶ engaging ▶ evolving

First published in 2015, reprinted in 2016, 2017, 2019.

Insight Publications Pty Ltd
3/350 Charman Road
Cheltenham VIC 3192
Australia
Tel: +61 3 8571 4950
Fax: +61 3 8571 0257
Email: books@insightpublications.com.au

www.insightpublications.com.au

National Library of Australia Cataloguing-in-Publication entry:

Bladen, Victoria, author.
William Shakespeare's Measure for measure / Victoria Bladen.
9781925316001 (paperback)
Insight text guide.
Includes bibliographical references.
For secondary school age.
Shakespeare, William, 1564–1616. Measure for measure.
Shakespeare, William, 1564–1616—Criticism and interpretation.
822.33

Other ISBNs:
9781925316018 (digital)
9781925316025 (bundle: print + digital)

Cover design: The Modern Art Production Group

Printed in Australia

Author's dedication: This book is dedicated to my sister Cassandra, with love

contents

CHARACTER MAP

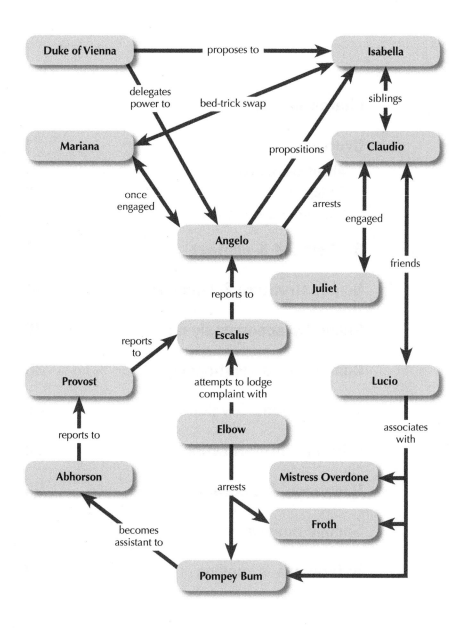

OVERVIEW

William Shakespeare (1564–1616) is one of the most renowned figures of the English literary Renaissance (also known as the 'early modern period'). His dramatic and poetic work, written during an intensely productive period from the late sixteenth to the early seventeenth century, has proved capable of enduring well beyond his own time and place. Translated into many languages and adapted for film, television, ballet, opera, graphic novels and online games, Shakespeare's work has evolved into a cultural phenomenon, meaningful and compelling for audiences of different periods and cultures.

Measure for Measure was first performed at court before James I in 1604. More serious in tone than many of Shakespeare's other comedies, it is often classified as a tragicomedy and considered one of Shakespeare's 'problem plays' (a small group of his plays that are not easily categorised as comedy or tragedy). *Measure for Measure* raises questions about power, sexuality and justice. This guide will help you to navigate your way through the play, organise your thinking, and write on the text.

Keep in mind that *Measure for Measure* is a *play*, intended as a performance on stage. If you have the opportunity to see the play performed you will gain a deeper understanding of its shape, characters, dramatic action and language. Alternatively, why not organise your own play reading with a group of friends? Viewing screen adaptations will also add to your understanding of the play; however, this is not a substitute for close reading of the text.

About the author

Shakespeare was born in 1564, when Elizabeth I was on the throne, and died in 1616, when James I was king. Born into a middle-class family in Stratford-upon-Avon, in Warwickshire, William was the son of John Shakespeare, a glove-maker and landowner, and his wife Mary, a gentleman's daughter. Shakespeare received an education from the King's New School in Stratford, but never attended university. As a young man he fell in love with Anne Hathaway, and they were married in 1582 after Anne became pregnant; the child, Susanna, was born six months after the wedding. Twins, Hamnet and Judith, were born in 1585; Hamnet died when he was a child. Subsequently, the marriage appears to have broken down.

In the late 1580s, Shakespeare moved to London and began his career as a playwright. He joined a theatre company called The Lord Chamberlain's Men (also briefly known as Lord Hunsdon's Men), under the patronage of the Lord Chamberlain. The ensemble produced plays that were performed at a venue called the Theatre. He acted, wrote plays for and shared in the profits of the theatre company. When the lease over the land on which the Theatre was built expired in 1597 and a dispute with the landlord arose, Shakespeare and his colleagues dismantled the wooden building, took it across the river and reassembled it at Bankside, south of the Thames. This theatre, renamed the Globe, opened in 1599. From late 1609, Shakespeare's company also used an indoor theatre, Blackfriars, for winter performances, while the Globe was used in the summer. In London today, a close replica of the Globe stands near the original site. To this has been added a new theatre, the Sam Wanamaker Playhouse, modelled on early modern indoor theatre designs.

When James I came to the throne in 1603 he became the patron of the theatre company of which Shakespeare was part owner; the company was therefore renamed the King's Men. The king recognised the huge potential of the theatre to reach many people; in this regard, theatre then was like television or the internet now.

Synopsis

Measure for Measure has a darker mood than other Shakespearean comedies you may have encountered. It raises some difficult issues, which has led to its characterisation as a 'problem' comedy (see further discussion in 'Genre, Structure & Language'). Vienna is presented as a society with a dysfunctional political state and an unbalanced attitude to sexuality. Women are traded as commodities in the flourishing brothels of the city or left vulnerable and unmarried for lack of a dowry. No wonder, then, that Isabella seeks to escape these risks by becoming a nun.

The Duke avoids his political responsibility by delegating power to his deputy Angelo, even though Escalus seems the wiser choice. Angelo applies without mercy the strict laws governing sexuality. The plight of Claudio, sentenced to death for premarital sex with his fiancée Juliet, is a consequence of this harsh state policy. Angelo, outwardly Puritan and restrained, is revealed as hypocritical and corrupt. He abuses his power by imposing a stark choice on Isabella, who comes to plead for her brother's life: if she wishes to save Claudio she must sleep with Angelo. The Duke, who secretly mediates between the various characters, attempts to rectify the situation by proposing a bed-trick whereby Mariana, Angelo's former fiancée, will be a substitute for Isabella. What is distinctly lacking in Vienna is a sense of measure: moderation in its attitude to sexuality and the exercise of power.

In the first act, we are introduced to a Vienna with a prosperous trade in prostitution, where Mistress Overdone and Pompey Bum's business has been thriving. Although there are strict laws against licentiousness (lewdness or unrestrained sexuality), the Duke of Vienna has not enforced them, and now feels that matters are out of control. He delegates to his strict deputy Angelo, ostensibly to apply the laws, then disguises himself as a friar to spy on Angelo and observe what happens in Vienna. Under the new strict regime, Claudio is arrested on the charge of premarital sex and is sentenced to death. He sends for his sister Isabella, to use her skills in rhetoric to plead for his life. Isabella, a pious and chaste woman, was about to enter the sisterhood of Saint Clare as a novice nun but must delay this to help her brother.

In the second act, Angelo and Escalus represent different approaches to the exercise of power. When Elbow the constable attempts to bring charges against Froth and Pompey Bum, his confusing malapropisms (incorrect words that sound similar to the words he intends) leave Angelo exasperated. Angelo leaves the case in Escalus' capable hands and Escalus lets both the accused off with a warning. Isabella pleads with Angelo to save Claudio, while Angelo finds himself aroused by Isabella's virtue and presents her with a disturbing choice: to save her brother, Isabella must sleep with Angelo. Isabella refuses and resolves to tell Claudio of Angelo's hypocritical demand, confident that her brother would not want her to compromise her virtue. Meanwhile, the Duke has learned of Claudio's plight.

The third act sees the disguised Duke visit Claudio to prepare him for death. Isabella informs Claudio of Angelo's indecent proposal and is angry when he begs her to save his life by giving in to Angelo. The Duke overhears and proposes a solution whereby Angelo's former fiancée Mariana will take the place of Isabella through a 'bed-trick'. Meanwhile Pompey and Mistress Overdone are arrested. Lucio unwittingly slanders the disguised Duke, and Mistress Overdone informs on Lucio for failing to marry a woman, Kate Keepdown, after she became pregnant by him. Escalus gives his positive opinion on the Duke. The act ends with the Duke, in soliloquy, reflecting on how rulers should exercise power.

In Act 4, after the bed-trick has taken place, the Duke expects Angelo to reverse the order for Claudio's execution. However, Angelo orders it to go ahead and that Claudio's head be produced as evidence. The Duke then proposes that the head of Barnardine, another prisoner due to be executed, replace that of Claudio. However, Barnardine refuses to be executed as he has been drinking all night. Luckily another prisoner, the pirate Ragozine, has just died; his head is substituted for Claudio's. The Duke withholds from Isabella the knowledge that Claudio is still alive. The Duke writes to Escalus and Angelo, announcing his return, and Angelo reflects on his guilt. Friar Peter takes Isabella and Mariana to the gates of the city to prepare for the Duke's arrival.

In the final act the Duke returns in his own guise at the gates of Vienna where Isabella publicly denounces Angelo and asks for justice. The Duke pretends at first to disbelieve her, ordering that Isabella be arrested and sending for Friar Lodowick (the Duke's alter ego). Mariana also levels accusations at Angelo. Friar Lodowick appears, denounces Angelo and is unveiled by Lucio. Angelo confesses, asking for death as his sentence. Mariana and Isabella plead for the Duke to show mercy, which he does. However, Angelo must marry Mariana, and Lucio is to marry Kate Keepdown. In a swift yet problematical conclusion, the Duke proposes marriage to Isabella after finally revealing to her that Claudio is alive. From Isabella we hear a deafening silence.

Character summaries

The Duke of Vienna, Vincentio; Friar Lodowick

The Duke is an enigmatic figure. He feels he has been lax as a ruler in not enforcing Vienna's laws so he delegates his power to Angelo, then disguises himself as a friar to observe what happens.

Isabella

Isabella, Claudio's sister, is a chaste and pious woman whose plans to enter the sisterhood of Saint Clare as a novice nun have to be postponed in order to plead for Claudio's life.

Angelo

A strict Puritan until he meets Isabella, Angelo is overcome with desire for her and demands that she sleep with him in order to save her brother's life.

Claudio

Claudio, Isabella's brother, is engaged to Juliet, who is pregnant to him. He is arrested under the new strict regime of Angelo's government, on the charge of premarital sex, and sentenced to death.

Escalus

Escalus is a lord and a wise counsellor to the Duke.

Lucio

Moving between upper and lower circles of Viennese society, Lucio is an often comic figure. He refuses to marry Kate Keepdown when she becomes pregnant to him. He is also careless with his words – his slanders of the Duke come back to haunt him.

Juliet

Juliet is Claudio's fiancée and is pregnant to him.

Mariana

Mariana, Angelo's former mistress, is instrumental in the bed-trick.

Elbow

A constable, Elbow is a comic figure whose speech is full of malapropisms.

Mistress Overdone

Mistress Overdone, a brothel manager, is distressed at the new proclamation closing all the brothels in the suburbs.

Pompey Bum

Also a brothel manager, Pompey Bum is an associate of Mistress Overdone.

Froth

Froth is a gentleman who frequents the brothels.

Barnardine

Barnardine is one of Claudio's fellow prisoners, sentenced to death.

Abhorson

Abhorson is the executioner.

Provost

The provost is a justice and a government officer.

Francisca

Francisca is a nun of Saint Clare.

Friar Thomas and Friar Peter

These are the friars through whom the Duke organises his disguise.

BACKGROUND & CONTEXT

The play's setting

Measure for Measure is set in early modern Vienna. The Duke's name – Vincentio – suggests that Shakespeare may have had in mind the historical figure of Vincenzo Gonzago, Duke of Mantua (1587–1612), who spent time in Vienna and whose wife became a nun after they divorced. In Shakespeare's time Vienna was ruled by the powerful Habsburg family and was part of the Holy Roman Empire, which covered a large territory in Europe. Vienna was Catholic, in contrast to Shakespeare's England, which was predominantly Protestant. Although the play is set in Vienna, many of its themes reflect aspects of life in Shakespeare's London. The play also explores ideas of interest to James I, such as the exercise of power, on which he had reflected in his publication *Basilikon Doron* (1603).

Most of the scenes are set in various locations around Vienna, except for 4.1 and 4.5, which take place outside the city. The locations include the court, the nunnery of Saint Clare, a monastery, the streets and the city gates; however, most of the scenes take place at the prison, which reflects the themes of the play.

Vienna is presented as a place of extreme contrasts. On the one hand there is the new strict regime under Angelo that seeks to control all forms of licentiousness. We also have the chaste figure of Isabella, who is about to enter the nunnery as a novice. On the other hand, there is the thriving world of prostitution, and the colourful characters that inhabit the brothels of the city.

Shakespeare's historical context

Power

In Shakespeare's England there was no democracy. The political system was a monarchy and complete power resided with the monarch, who inherited their position by birth, not by a system of voting. Furthermore, the king or queen usually held the crown for life; upon their death their heir inherited the throne. The ordinary person had no political power and was subject to the will of the monarch. This meant that people were particularly vulnerable to the abuse of power. In the play, the arrest and near-execution of Claudio reflects how the state had power over the most intimate aspects of the individual subject's life.

The dubious surveillance and interference by the Duke raises questions about the extent to which rulers should be involved in the lives of their subjects. In Shakespeare's time, the government was involved in surveillance through a network of spies as one of its mechanisms for maintaining power. It was dangerous to speak out against the monarch or resist the religious or political status quo. The Duke's disguise and spying activities resonate with the way power was exercised in the early modern period.

Sexuality and the physical body

Early modern attitudes to sexuality were governed by religious ideology. Humanity was seen as 'fallen', in accordance with the Christian narrative of the Fall, which related how Adam and Eve were expelled from the Garden of Eden after they ate fruit from the tree of knowledge. The body was thought to be easily susceptible to sin, and the ordinary sexual functions of the body, which in modern Western society are regarded as perfectly natural, were often a cause of shame and anxiety. Sexuality was only permissible within marriage, and even then there were restrictions. There was also a lack of medical knowledge about how sexually transmitted diseases were transferred and there were no cures. This contributed to the association of sexuality with immorality and sin.

Puritanism

England was predominantly Protestant at the time Shakespeare wrote *Measure for Measure*. In the sixteenth century, Protestantism had emerged as a 'protest' to some of the ideology and practices of the Catholic Church, and it became a separate branch of the Christian Church. This resulted in much conflict and bloodshed across Europe and within England. In the Tudor period, Henry VIII broke away from the Catholic Church based in Rome, creating himself as Supreme Head of the Church of England.

While Protestants saw themselves as having reformed aspects of Catholic doctrine and practice, another group within Protestantism, the Puritans, wanted further reforms. The conflict between Protestants and Puritans became a significant development contributing to the English Civil War, which broke out towards the middle of the seventeenth century. Angelo's character traits, his strictness and harsh application of the law, evoke those of the Puritans. Some Puritans advocated extreme sentences, such as capital punishment, for sex outside of marriage. The Puritans were also often hostile to the newly emerged public theatres of Shakespeare's time; they saw them as immoral, and associated them with the brothels and bear-baiting venues near the theatres, in the 'Liberties': the peripheral areas outside the jurisdiction of central London.

Humours

The human body was thought to be comprised of four humours (fluids): blood, choler, melancholy and phlegm. Different characteristics were associated with each of these substances and their proportions in a person dictated their personality. Imbalances in the humours were believed to cause adverse health effects and particular behaviour. In Shakespeare's work there are often references to the humours affecting behaviour or personality. For example, Isabella refers to 'a choleric word' (2.2.155), meaning a word spoken in anger, arising from an excess of choler.

The position of women

In the early modern period women were perceived as socially and intellectually inferior to men. It was assumed that women belonged in the home and they generally could not own property; they were considered the property of men. These ideas about women rendered them particularly vulnerable. Unmarried pregnant women, like Juliet, were likely to be cast out from society. Poor women were at risk of having to resort to prostitution to survive. When Angelo abuses his power by attempting to pressure Isabella into having sex with him, he is taking advantage not only of his power as a ruler over a subject, but also of his power as a man over a woman. According to the Christian narrative, women were created from men (Eve from Adam's rib). Isabella refers to this idea when she responds to Angelo's sexual advance in 2.4 by stating 'Help heaven! Men their creation mar / In profiting by them' (2.4.133–4); in other words, men should not abuse what has been created from them.

Death

In the early modern period there was much philosophical reflection on death and the idea of dying well, that is, dying with the soul prepared. Life expectancy was low, rates of death in childbirth and child mortality were high and there was a lack of medical knowledge about disease and hygiene. Thus death was ever present. Life on earth was often considered ephemeral and of little worth in comparison with the eternal life of the soul – the long afterlife that Christian ideology envisaged. In art and literature there was the idea of the *memento mori*: objects, images or sayings that were intended to remind people about their mortality and to live life accordingly.

The notion of the art of dying, of being mentally and spiritually prepared for death, arises at several moments in *Measure for Measure*. The Duke visits Claudio to prepare him for death, so that he is mentally resigned to what he must face. Barnardine manages to prolong his life by arguing with his jailers that he is not yet prepared for death, since he has been up drinking all night. When Isabella visits Claudio and tells him of the choice Angelo has given her, Claudio conveys the human fear of death through his vivid imagery. Between them the characters present a range of ideas about death.

The seven deadly sins

In Shakespeare's period, human failings were often categorised as the 'seven deadly sins'. These were: pride, gluttony, lust, wrath, sloth, avarice and envy. Humans were supposed to be moderate and temperate in their behaviour and appetites, an idea originating with Aristotle and adopted by Christian ideology. Of these sins, the play is primarily concerned with lust.

Classical mythology

The English Renaissance period (from the late sixteenth century to 1660) was one of intense literary production that included a revival of interest in classical Greek and Roman literature. English Renaissance literature commonly alludes to classical mythology, tales of gods and goddesses. Since there were restrictions on referring to the Christian God in the early modern theatre, classical mythology was a useful way of doing so through analogy. For example, the classical god Jove (Jupiter or Zeus), the father of the gods, could be used to refer to the Christian God (as in 2.2.135).

Publication history

There are no surviving draft manuscripts, notes or diaries left by Shakespeare so scholars have to piece together other evidence to determine a publication date. The play was first performed in 1604 and is believed to have been written earlier that year. The only surviving edition is the 1623 First Folio.

In crafting his play, Shakespeare drew elements of his plot from earlier sources, such as Giovanbattista Giraldi Cinthio's *Hecatommithi* (1565) and George Whetstone's *Promos and Cassandra* (1578). The motif of the disguised ruler appears in other early modern plays such as Thomas Middleton's *The Phoenix* (1603) and John Marston's *The Malcontent* (1603).

The title, *Measure for Measure*, is a reference to a biblical passage on Jesus' Sermon on the Mount: 'Judge not, that ye be not judged. / For with what judgment ye judge, ye shall be judged: and with what measure ye mete, it shall be measured to you again' (Matthew 7:1–2). The passage suggests that God will ensure judges are treated in the same manner as they judge others. However, the play raises various questions about exercising justice and mercy.

GENRE, STRUCTURE & LANGUAGE

Genre

In the 1623 First Folio, the editors divided the plays into three genres: comedies, tragedies and histories. We still use these general classifications, although with qualifications and in the knowledge that genres often intersect. When the generic term 'comedy' is used, it doesn't mean that a play is necessarily intended to be funny (although it may well contain humorous scenes) but rather that the play resolves conflict at the end, with separated couples coming together. Whereas a tragedy ends with death, comedy generally ends with marriage (or at least betrothal).

Some of Shakespeare's comedies share certain characteristics with the tragedies, and are thus described as tragicomedies. Although their endings present ostensible resolutions to the conflicts and issues explored in the plays, certain aspects remain unresolved, or problematical. Furthermore, there may be losses along the way that can never be retrieved. *Measure for Measure* is a tragicomedy. It is also often described as a 'problem play' and grouped with *All's Well That Ends Well* and *Troilus and Cressida* because they are not as light-hearted as other Shakespearean comedies, instead presenting us with more serious and intense subject matter.

In *Measure for Measure* some of the couples united at the end are unsuited and incompatible; that is, the generic requirement of marriage appears forced. The Duke's proposal to Isabella is unsettling; Isabella does not love the Duke, and marriage is completely contrary to her identity and the way she wants to live her life. Questions also remain as to how successful the marriage of Angelo and Mariana will be, when it has been forced on him and he did not treat her well initially. There are similar doubts about the success of Lucio's marriage. While Claudio and Juliet are united, the trials they have undergone have been extreme. These factors, and the intense, serious dilemmas raised by the play, contribute to its generic classification as a tragicomedy and 'problem play'.

Structure

The play is divided into five acts, constructed of multiple scenes that oscillate between the world of the court and that of the low figures, yet most often centred on the prison. The first part of the play, comprising the first two acts, presents the serious dilemmas and threats that the new punitive regime presents. Its tone is intense as it pits the various characters and their motivations against one another and draws us into what appears to be an unresolvable situation. In the first act we learn of the arrest of Claudio, for premarital sex with his fiancée, and of the new proclamation shutting down the brothels in the suburbs. The second act shifts to the relationship between Claudio, who faces death, and his sister Isabella, who confronts the moral dilemma of whether to sacrifice her chastity to save her brother.

The second part of the play, from Act 3 onwards, focuses on the machinations of the Duke in disguise, as he works to create solutions to the problems raised in the first section of the play. This section has a more folktale-like quality, whereby solutions to the various dilemmas in the first part are resolved by a series of substitutions and less realistic plot devices. The bed-trick (also a feature of *All's Well That Ends Well*) requires a certain suspension of disbelief. It also seems fantastical and comical that the prisoner Barnardine has been able to avoid execution, purely through his ability to talk his way out of it.

In the latter part of the play, particularly from Act 4, the scenes become shorter, making the shifts between the different groups of characters more rapid. This accelerates the pace of the play, creating momentum and greater dramatic tension as it builds towards the climax at the gates of the city in the longer scene of 5.1.

Note how several scenes begin as if in the middle of a conversation. For example, at the beginning of 1.4, the Duke appears to be responding to an earlier suggestion by Friar Thomas that the Duke is relinquishing his power because of love. Similarly at the beginning of 1.5, the conversation between Isabella and the nun Francisca appears to have already started before we become witnesses to the scene. The effect of this structure is to create the illusion of an authentic world that exists beyond what we see taking place on stage.

Language

Shakespeare was a gifted wordsmith, inventing many new words and playing on the multiple meanings of a word. Shifts in a conversation often hinge on a word used in one sense by one character, then in a different sense by another. His language can be difficult when encountered for the first time; some words that were common at the time are now unfamiliar. Other words may be familiar but their meaning has changed over time, which can be misleading – the 'Key vocabulary' sections will help you with this. Shakespeare's syntax (the order of words) can also be challenging. Sometimes it can be useful for you to rewrite conversations or scenes in your own words, once you have studied the vocabulary lists to understand unfamiliar words and phrases.

It is more important to try to gain an overall sense of a passage than to understand each component. Watching a play or a film will help you, since body language, gesture and tone of voice all add meaning. Also, reading the play more than once will help; with each reading you will gain new insights and greater understanding of how Shakespeare's language works.

You will notice Shakespeare's frequent use of metaphors and similes to describe people, emotions and events. For example in 1.3, Claudio refers to the legal penalties which, up until now, have not been enforced; he imagines them as 'like unscoured armour, hung by th'wall' (1.3.53). Similarly, he refers to the 'drowsy and neglected act' (1.3.56), personifying the legislation as someone who has gone to sleep because of disuse. Shakespeare also uses personification when the Duke says 'liberty plucks justice by the nose' (1.4.30), imagining the abstract qualities of liberty and justice as human figures, liberty insulting and challenging justice. Such use of figurative language was common in Renaissance literature; it adds depth and complexity to the dramatic language through the mental images that the words evoke.

Comedy is an important aspect of Shakespeare's language, particularly in the speeches of the low characters. In *Measure for Measure*, you will encounter a lot of bawdy language: words and expressions that refer to sexual activity and sexually transmitted diseases. Humour also arises from the malapropisms of Elbow the constable. Many of the conversations may be difficult to follow as they pun on expressions and words that are no longer familiar to us. You will need to refer to the 'Key vocabulary' sections to understand the innuendo.

Sometimes Shakespeare's word play draws on similar-sounding words or phrases. At other times, he plays with opposite ideas, for example where Claudio observes that his 'restraint' (1.3.9), his arrest, has come 'from too much liberty' (1.3.10) in giving in to his natural desire for his fiancée.

As you are reading the play, note the rhythm of the language. Most of the upper-class characters generally speak in verse, while the lower-class characters speak in prose. The verse lines are in iambic pentameter – there are five 'beats' or stresses to the line, with unstressed syllables in between. This pattern gives a sense of overall order. Changes between prose and verse can be used to create particular effects. For example, Lucio sometimes speaks in prose and sometimes in verse. This conveys the way that he moves between upper and lower circles. When the Duke appears as himself, he speaks in verse, but when disguised as the friar he speaks in prose. Note that, in 3.1, once Lucio leaves and the Duke is by himself, he reverts to verse again (3.1.463–7).

You may also notice that some lines seem to 'stand out' from the text as memorable quotations that could be used outside of the play, for example where Lucio says, 'Our doubts are traitors, / And make us lose the good we oft might win / By fearing to attempt' (1.5.84–6). In Shakespeare's time, proverbs and aphorisms were popular; these were short sayings, usually with a didactic function (trying to teach a moral lesson). The more educated audience members often took notes of useful lines they heard at the theatre, later adding them to their commonplace books (compilations of useful sayings).

SCENE-BY-SCENE ANALYSIS

Act 1

1.1 Summary: *The Duke of Vienna delegates his power to Angelo, claiming that Angelo will be strict in applying the laws, thus rectifying the Duke's laxity.*

The Duke announces to Escalus that he has delegated his power to Angelo, even though Escalus appears to be the wiser choice. Note how the alliteration linking 'mortality' and 'mercy' conveys the way lives hang in the balance, controlled by those in power (1.1.46). The Duke wants to test his deputy; Angelo asks for a greater test. In this regard, Angelo is like Isabella: both display a type of masochistic excess in restraining themselves. The Duke asks Angelo to apply the law as he sees fit.

1.2 Summary: *We are introduced to Lucio; the bawds Mistress Overdone and Pompey Bum comment on Angelo's new strict regime, with brothels in the suburbs to be closed; Claudio has been arrested for premarital sex with his fiancée.*

Lucio enters with two gentlemen, discussing a current political conflict with the King of Hungary. There follows some humorous banter and word play before Mistress Overdone, a brothel owner, enters. Lucio refers to the sexually transmitted diseases he has caught from sleeping with her prostitutes. Mistress Overdone tells them that Claudio, whose fiancée Juliet is pregnant, is to be executed in three days. Pompey Bum tells of the new proclamation in Vienna that all brothels in the suburbs must be shut down, although ironically the brothels in the city are to be left alone, so the trade will continue. Mistress Overdone is dismayed at the loss of her livelihood.

1.3 Summary: *Claudio reflects on his offence and asks Lucio to send for his sister, Isabella.*

Claudio enters and explains the cause of his arrest. Although he is engaged to Juliet, they are not yet married, and he has broken the law prohibiting premarital sex. Claudio asks Lucio to find Isabella, his sister, to tell her of his plight and request that she use her powers of rhetoric to plead for him.

1.4 Summary: *The Duke speaks to Friar Thomas of his motives for delegating power to Angelo.*

In conversation with Friar Thomas, the Duke claims that he has 'ever loved the life removed' (1.4.9): the contemplative life away from the active life of politics. Despite telling Angelo that he is travelling to Poland, in fact the Duke plans to remain in Vienna in disguise. He feels responsible for Vienna becoming licentious and lawless; he has not enforced the laws, yet feels it would be inconsistent of him to suddenly do so. Consequently he has appointed Angelo, who he knows to be strict in nature (although later we find that the Duke knew of Angelo's poor treatment of Mariana). The Duke proposes to dress in disguise as a friar; his role thus shifts to one of surveillance.

1.5 Summary: *Isabella is about to enter the sisterhood of Saint Clare when Lucio arrives to inform her of her brother's plight.*

Isabella asks the nun Francisca about the restraints the nuns are subject to. Even though these involve chastity, poverty and silence, Isabella wishes for 'a more strict restraint' (1.5.4). The word restraint recalls Claudio's earlier use of the word in 1.3. Lucio enters and the nun advises Isabella to speak with him. Once Isabella is sworn in as a nun, there will be restrictions on speaking with men. Lucio relates how Claudio is in prison, the Duke is gone and Angelo governs in his place. He urges Isabella to use her power of rhetoric to save Claudio; she is at first doubtful but then resolves to try.

Key point

The Duke's delegation of power would have been regarded as problematic by Shakespeare's audience. Rulers were believed to be God's representatives on earth and were expected to govern responsibly, not delegate their power. In the tragedy *King Lear* Shakespeare presents the disastrous consequences of a monarch giving away his right to rule.

Key vocabulary

Pregnant (1.1.11): knowledgeable, well-informed

Doth (1.1.34): does

Thou (1.1.45): you

Leavened (1.1.55): carefully considered; developed

Aves (1.1.75): shouts of welcome

Bottom of my place (1.1.83): full extent of my position

Composition (1.2.2): agreement; settlement

Kersey (1.2.33): type of plain, coarse cloth

Sciatica (1.2.58): pain in the hip; believed to be a symptom of syphilis

Sweat (1.2.83): sweating sickness

Groping for trouts in a peculiar river (1.2.90): sex

Houses (1.2.96): brothels

Tapster (1.2.109): barman

Ravin (1.3.14): devour

Lief (1.3.18): willingly

Foppery (1.3.18): folly

Dower (1.3.35): dowry

Coffer (1.3.36): protective enclosure

Zodiacs (1.3.54): years

Tickle (1.3.58): insecurely

Tick-tack (1.3.77): game; sex

Prithee (1.4.48): 'pray thee'; ask

Precise (1.4.53): Puritan; strict

Votarists (1.5.5): those bound by religious vows

Lapwing (1.5.34): plover, type of bird associated with amorous intrigue and deceit

Enskied (1.5.36): heavenly

Foison (1.5.45): harvest

Tilth and husbandry (1.5.46): ploughing and cultivation; sex

Q What are the key issues raised in the first act?

Q How does Claudio respond to his arrest and why?

Act 2

2.1 Summary: *Angelo believes the law should be strictly applied but Escalus cautions that moderation is best; Elbow attempts to convey his allegations against Pompey and Froth for leading his wife astray, but his malapropisms confuse Angelo and Escalus; Escalus is left to administer judgement and he lets both accused off with a warning.*

Angelo uses the metaphor of the scarecrow to describe the law. If the scarecrow never moves, then even birds of prey will eventually just use it as a perch; likewise the inactive law won't be a source of terror. However, Escalus cautions that Angelo should only 'cut a little' (2.1.6) and not be too zealous in applying the law. Escalus wishes to save Claudio, and wisely asks Angelo to consider whether he himself could have transgressed the law, in other circumstances. That is, Escalus warns him not to be hypocritical. Angelo admits that he is making an example of Claudio. He instructs the Provost to execute Claudio the next day. The immediacy of the sentence invites the audience to question his judgement.

Elbow arrives, having arrested Froth and Pompey. His speech is full of malapropisms, thus he confuses Angelo and Escalus. Pompey also confuses the situation and suggests that Elbow's wife has been frequently at the brothel. The conversation is full of bawdy innuendo that Shakespeare's audience would have been alert to.

Angelo, in frustration, leaves Escalus to sort it out. Escalus, although aware that Pompey is a bawd and that Master Froth has been spending time in the brothels, lets both off with a warning, demonstrating his pragmatic approach to administering justice. Elbow, misunderstanding Escalus' directive to the accused to 'continue' (2.1.187), triumphantly believes this to be a punishment. The scene ends with Escalus expressing sympathy for Claudio, while recognising that mercy cannot always be shown.

2.2 Summary: *Isabella pleads with Angelo to save Claudio, reminding him of the need for rulers to be merciful; Angelo finds himself aroused by Isabella's virtue and asks her to return the next day.*

The Provost expresses concern that Claudio will die for something that many others are also guilty of. He questions Angelo but is disregarded. Lucio enters with Isabella, who appeals to Angelo. She expresses her inner turmoil at having to plead for her brother when, she says, his sin is 'a vice that most I do abhor, / And most desire should meet the blow of justice' (2.2.40–1). That she is only partly committed to the attempt to save her brother is indicated by the way she gives up the cause so quickly. Lucio persuades her to try again. Throughout Isabella's appeal to Angelo, both Lucio and the Provost look on and wish her success.

Note the joined lines where Isabella and Angelo complete each other's half-lines. For example, Isabella's 'Must he needs die?' is followed by Angelo's 'Maiden, no remedy' (2.2.62–3); a similar effect is created a few lines later (2.2.71–2). Shakespeare often uses this effect where he wants to indicate specific relationships between two characters. Here, it anticipates Angelo becoming attracted to Isabella.

Note also that Angelo suggests he has no *inclination* to save Claudio (2.2.68), which implies he has *power* to do so if he wished; later, though, he contradicts this by saying he has no choice (2.2.101). Angelo says it is too late in any event, as Claudio has already been sentenced. Isabella argues that it is mercy that best becomes a ruler (2.2.76–80), which has parallels with Portia's famous speech in Shakespeare's *The Merchant of Venice* (beginning 'The quality of mercy is not strained; / It droppeth as the gentle rain from heaven', 4.1.182–3). Isabella points out that if Angelo's and Claudio's positions had been reversed, Claudio would have shown mercy; yet Angelo continues to dismiss her. Isabella asks Angelo how mankind would be if God showed the lack of mercy that Angelo is showing.

There is force in Angelo's claim that it is the law, not he, that condemns Claudio (2.2.101). The Duke bears some responsibility for the harsh laws that are in place; only he has the power to change them. Note the way in which Angelo personifies the law, describing it as a person who has slept and now wakes (2.2.112–15); this gives the idea greater impact as it creates an image in the mind of the audience, rather than simply describing an abstract quality.

Isabella then argues that rulers should not *utilise* all the power they wield, as if they were 'Jove' – an example of how reference to the classical gods allows Shakespeare to get around the restrictions regarding direct mention of the Christian God. Shakespeare's audience would have understood that 'Jove' referred to God. Finally Isabella argues that Angelo should put himself in Claudio's shoes. She asks him not to be hypocritical, to 'ask your heart what it doth know / That's like my brother's fault' (2.2.162–3). Angelo asks Isabella to return tomorrow. Once alone, Angelo wonders at the desire she has aroused in him.

2.3 Summary: *The Duke, disguised as a friar, attends the prison and learns of Claudio's plight from the Provost.*

2.4 Summary: *Angelo proposes to Isabella that if she will sleep with him, he will save Claudio. Isabella is horrified and points out Angelo's hypocrisy.*

Angelo's soliloquy reveals his inner state. When Isabella enters, he adds a sexual tone in responding to her plain statements. He puts a hypothetical situation to her. Would she trade her body to save her brother? She does not grasp the meaning of his innuendo at first and assumes that by giving up her body he means death. 'I had rather give my body than my soul', she claims (2.4.57). Angelo's observation, that her 'sense pursues not' his (2.4.78), implies sense as both meaning and physical desire.

Isabella claims that it would be better for her brother to die than for her to risk her eternal soul. Once Angelo has made his demand more bluntly, Isabella points out his hypocrisy in condemning Claudio for the same sin that Angelo is now proposing. Isabella threatens to inform against Angelo; however, he relies on his superior position and his reputation: who will believe her against him? Furthermore, he threatens that if she does not 'consent to' his 'sharp appetite' he will ensure Claudio suffers a drawn-out death (2.4.170). Once Angelo leaves, Isabella's soliloquy reveals her faith in her brother. She is sure he would rather die than allow her to lose her honour. She resolves to tell him, so he can prepare for death.

Key point

The issue of whether or not to show mercy is a difficult one. Escalus expresses this when he reflects: 'Mercy is not itself that oft looks so, / Pardon is still the nurse of second woe' (2.1.282–3). He recognises that showing mercy in one instance may simply encourage further offending; mercy needs to be shown sparingly. Angelo argues that the act of showing 'justice' is merciful, as it considers those wronged by an offence and prevents future offences (2.2.123–7). Yet, as Isabella reminds Angelo, rulers need to remember how God has shown mercy to sinful humanity, and that they should imitate God (2.2.95–9). The challenge is to know when to punish and when to show mercy.

Key vocabulary

Pilgrimage (2.1.39): limit of life's journey

Out at elbow (2.1.63): disconcerted

Parcel bawd (2.1.65): part-time brothel manager

Hot-house (2.1.68): bath-house; brothel

Stewed prunes (2.1.92–3): dish available in brothels; used to treat syphilis; euphemism for scrotum; pun on 'stews' (brothels)

Fruit-dish (2.1.94): vagina

Stones (2.1.109): testicles

Caitiff (2.1.184): rascal; knave

Geld; splay (2.1.229): castrate; spay

Drabs (2.1.233): prostitutes

Cipher of a function (2.1.52): meaningless role

Forfeit (2.2.90): lost life (to the law)

Pelting (2.2.136): paltry

Fantastic (2.2.145): illusory; foolish

Choleric (2.2.155): angry; full of choler

Sense (2.2.168): desire

Sicles (2.2.175): coins

Lightness (2.2.200): promiscuity

Strumpet (2.2.213): prostitute; promiscuous woman

Blistered her report (2.3.12): tarnished her reputation

Meet (2.3.33): appropriate

Boot (2.4.11): advantage

Enshield (2.4.84): concealed

Destined livery (2.4.145): uniform (of women's frailty)

Prompture (2.4.187): urging

Q Identify all of Elbow's malapropisms in 2.1, using the vocabulary list on the previous page. What is he trying to say and why is the effect humorous?

Q Analyse 2.4, a key scene. What arguments does Angelo use and how does Isabella respond?

Act 3

3.1 Summary: *The Duke, in disguise, visits Claudio to prepare him for death; Isabella tells Claudio of Angelo's proposal and is furious when Claudio pleads with her to save him; the Duke proposes the bed-trick plan. Pompey is arrested; Lucio refuses to provide bail and slanders the disguised Duke; Mistress Overdone is also arrested, and informs on Lucio for getting a woman pregnant yet failing to marry her. The Duke tests Escalus' loyalty and, in soliloquy, reflects on power.*

The Duke, disguised as a friar, uses his rhetoric to persuade Claudio to accept death. The Duke observes that man is never happy since when he's young he's poor, and when he's old, he doesn't have the health or beauty to enjoy his riches. Claudio is so persuaded by this speech that he says, 'I find I seek to die' (3.1.43). Isabella arrives and informs Claudio that she is fearful of telling him the only available solution lest he choose it. This contrasts with her optimism at the end of the previous scene. When Isabella does tell him of Angelo's demand, at first Claudio is adamant she will not do it, and he seems prepared for death. However, he quickly alters his position in a key speech articulating the human fear of death (3.1.129–43). A major source of his fear is the uncertainty of humanity's destination after death: 'and go we know not where' (3.1.129). Claudio does not appear to share the comforting certainty of Isabella's Christian belief in heaven. He argues that even the worst life imaginable is not as bad as death.

Isabella is furious at his about-face and curses him excessively, saying it were best he die quickly. Her response here seems particularly heartless. The Duke appears, speaking in prose rather than verse, which accords with his disguise. Isabella's and Claudio's speech also switches to prose here, reflecting their disempowered status at this point. The Duke assures Claudio of Angelo's good intentions, claiming Angelo intended merely to test Isabella's honour. After Claudio leaves, the Duke speaks with Isabella. Note the dramatic irony when Isabella expresses the wish that she could inform the Duke of Angelo's true nature (3.1.206–9). The Duke proposes a solution – the bed-trick, whereby Isabella will agree to Angelo's demand but Mariana will take Isabella's place in the bed under cover of darkness. Mariana was engaged to Angelo before her dowry was lost at sea with the life of Frederick, her brother, whereupon Angelo broke off the engagement.

Elbow and Pompey enter with officers. Elbow has arrested Pompey for being a bawd and thief, and the Duke rebukes him. Ironically, however, the Duke himself could be seen from one perspective as a type of bawd, having just arranged a sexual transaction between Mariana and Angelo. Elbow proposes to take Pompey before Angelo. Lucio refuses to provide bail for Pompey. Lucio wonders where the Duke might have gone, unknowingly guessing the truth when he states the Duke did 'usurp the beggary he was never born to' (3.1.375–6). Lucio reflects that it is impossible to extinguish licentiousness, wonders if Angelo is human, and, unaware of whom he is speaking with, slanders the Duke, suggesting that he is licentious and a drunkard. Note that once Lucio leaves, the Duke reverts to speaking in verse, as is appropriate for his upper-class status. He reflects on the power of slander and that even kings are not immune from it.

Escalus enters with Mistress Overdone, the Provost and officers. Mistress Overdone blames Lucio for informing on her and claims that Lucio himself got Mistress Kate Keepdown pregnant but has not married her. Escalus sends Mistress Overdone to prison and calls for Lucio. The 'friar' (Duke) asks Escalus his opinion of the Duke; he is spying on him to test his loyalty. Escalus answers positively and observes, among other things, that the Duke is 'a gentleman of all temperance' (3.1.515). The Duke reports that Claudio is resolved to die and Escalus reflects that Angelo is 'so severe' (3.1.531), he personifies Justice itself. While our contemporary notion of 'justice' encompasses 'fairness', in early modern culture 'justice' was generally harsh and juxtaposed with mercy. The act ends with the Duke reflecting on the nature of power. Note that the Duke changes from prose to verse for his lofty speech.

Key point

The Duke's persuasive speech to Claudio in 3.1 is an opportunity for Shakespeare to outline some reflections on the condition of mankind. Some of Shakespeare's audience would have taken notes on such philosophical observations and later written them up in their commonplace books.

Key vocabulary

Skyey (3.1.9): planetary (influences)

Leiger (3.1.59): resident ambassador

Vastidity (3.1.72): vastness

Prenzie (3.1.101): possibly an obscure heraldic term; alternatively a misprint for 'precise' (Puritan)

Bite the law by th'nose (3.1.119): mock the law

Perdurably fined (3.1.125): eternally punished

Assay (3.1.177): test

Affianced (3.1.229): betrothed

Scaled (3.1.270): weighed up

Moated grange (3.1.280): farmhouse surrounded by a moat

Bastard (3.1.288): wine (pun on illegitimacy)

Two usuries (3.1.290): referring to moneylending and prostitution

Maw (3.1.306): gullet/stomach

His neck will come to your waist (3.1.324): he will be hung (the noose is like the cord worn around a friar's waist)

Troth (3.1.339): in truth

Clack-dish (3.1.406): beggar's pot; vagina

Crochets (3.1.407): fanciful notions

Forswear (3.1.444): deny

Filling a bottle with a tundish (3.1.450): sex

Ungenitured (3.1.452): impotent

Untrussing (3.1.457): undressing

Calumny (3.1.464): slander

Q Analyse Claudio's speech at 3.1.129–43. What language and imagery does Shakespeare give Claudio to convey humanity's fear of death?

Q How does Isabella respond to Claudio's plea for her to save his life? What does her excessively hostile response reveal about her personality?

Act 4

4.1 Summary: *The Duke orchestrates plans for the bed-trick, liaising with Isabella and Mariana.*

The Duke speaks with Mariana and with Isabella, who informs him of the arrangements with Angelo. She is to enter via a vineyard which backs onto a walled garden. Isabella tells Mariana the plan. The Duke reflects on the position of rulers, subject to the slanders and fantasies of the people. Note the combined line at 4.1.75–6, which reflects Isabella and Mariana's joint project.

4.2 Summary: *Pompey is newly employed as the executioner's assistant. The Duke visits the prison and is surprised by Angelo's orders for the execution to go ahead and that Claudio's head be produced as evidence; the Duke asks the Provost to use Barnardine's head as a substitute.*

The Provost offers Pompey his freedom if he will accept the job of executioner's assistant. The executioner, Abhorson, arrives and Pompey seeks instructions. Claudio and Barnardine are due to die the next day.

Pompey indulges in word play with Abhorson, for example punning on 'hanging look' (4.2.33–4). Abhorson proposes to instruct Pompey in the trade and they exit. The Provost calls forth Claudio and Barnardine but the latter is asleep. The Duke enters in disguise, expecting Angelo to reverse Claudio's sentence (now that Angelo believes he has slept with Isabella), but the opposite happens. Angelo's note instructs the Provost to execute Claudio and Barnardine the next day and produce Claudio's head as evidence. Angelo's full nature is now evident to the Duke.

The Duke enquires after Barnardine and is advised that he has been a prisoner for nine years. The Provost describes him as a man unafraid of death. The Duke persuades the Provost to delay Claudio's death for four days and asks that Barnardine's head be substituted for Claudio's. The Duke (still disguised as the friar) then produces his seal to authorise the order and tells the Provost that the Duke will return within two days.

4.3 Summary: *Barnardine refuses to consent to being executed so it is decided to use Ragozine's head instead; the disguised Duke instructs Isabella to go with Friar Peter, not telling her Claudio is still alive; Lucio confesses he lied to escape a charge of getting a woman pregnant.*

Pompey, in soliloquy, reflects that being in the prison is just like being in Mistress Overdone's brothels, since many of her old customers are now in prison. The Duke arrives to hear Barnardine's confession before death; however, he 'will not consent to die' (4.3.54–5) because he's been drinking all night. His speech is humorous because it implies that the state cannot execute a prisoner unless they consent. The Provost informs the Duke that another prisoner, Ragozine, a pirate who bears some resemblance to Claudio, died of a fever. They decide to use his head as substitute for Claudio's. The (disguised) Duke proposes to write to Angelo informing him of the Duke's imminent return.

Isabella arrives, but the Duke – wanting to comfort her with the information at a later time of his choosing – does not tell her that Claudio is alive. He advises Isabella that the Duke will return tomorrow and that Escalus and Angelo are to meet him at the city gates. The Duke (still in disguise) organises for Friar Peter to bring Isabella before the Duke to accuse Angelo. Lucio enters; his description of 'the old fantastical duke of dark corners' (4.3.161–2) is particularly apt. Lucio states that he once appeared before the Duke on a charge of getting a woman pregnant, and confesses that he lied to escape being forced to marry the woman. This confession will come back to haunt him in the final scene.

4.4 Summary: *Escalus and Angelo anticipate the Duke's return; Angelo reflects on his guilt and why he had Claudio killed.*

Angelo and Escalus are confused by the Duke's instructions, particularly his direction for a proclamation to the citizens of Vienna that if anyone claims having suffered an injustice they should present their accusations when the Duke enters the gates. Escalus leaves and Angelo's soliloquy betrays his guilt. He fully recognises how his deed will appear: 'A deflowered maid, / And by an eminent body that enforced / The law against it!' (4.4.22–4). He weighs up whether Isabella is likely to accuse him, considering it improbable, given his reputation and the authority he wields. We also gain insight into why he ordered Claudio to be killed: Angelo feared that Claudio might have taken revenge against him. Angelo now doubts the wisdom of his actions.

4.5 Summary: *The Duke instructs Friar Peter to prepare for his return.*

4.6 Summary: *Isabella and Mariana prepare to carry out the Duke's instructions and Friar Peter arrives to take them to the gates.*

Isabella is uncomfortable about complying with the Duke's instructions. She would prefer to be able to state the truth directly. However the Duke plans to stage-manage events so that information is revealed at particular moments. Mariana urges Isabella to go along with the Duke's plans. The Duke also warns Isabella not to be concerned if he seems to speak against her at first and that it is only a means to an end. Friar Peter arrives to lead them to a good position from which to approach the gates.

Key point

In 4.2, although the Duke knows Angelo's nature, in speaking with the Provost he maintains the pretence that he believes Angelo to be virtuous (4.2.84–8). At the same time, he notes that were Angelo to be hypocritical, then 'were he tyrannous' (4.2.89). The Duke's nature is ambiguous throughout the play as he often veils his thoughts, withholding information until he deems the time right. Note how he allows Isabella to believe Claudio is dead, causing her suffering (4.3.118–19).

Key vocabulary

Circummured (4.1.28): walled around

Planchèd (4.1.30): made of planks

Ta'en a due (4.1.37): taken a careful (note)

Gyves (4.2.11): shackles

Time out of mind (4.2.15–16): longer than I can remember

Compound (4.2.23): agree on a sum

Mystery (4.2.29): craft, profession

Mealed (4.2.88): stained

Postern (4.2.94): back or side gate

Siege of justice (4.2.105): seat of justice

Celerity (4.2.118): swiftness

Signet (4.2.201): seal of authority

Anon (4.2.205): at once

House of profession (4.3.2): brothel

Peaches (4.3.11): impeaches, denounces

Billets (4.3.54): wooden sticks

Ward (4.3.62): cell

Gravel (4.3.63): stony

Perfect him withal (4.3.146): inform him

Woodman (4.3.166): hunter (of women)

Fain to forswear (4.3.175): eager to deny

Rotten medlar (4.3.176–7): rotten fruit; whore

Tongue (4.4.26): denounce

Ta'en (4.4.31): taken

Special drift (4.4.4): particular aim

Peradventure (4.6.6): by any chance

Q What observations about the exercise of power and justice does the Duke make in this act?

Q How is humour created through the figure of Barnardine?

Act 5

5.1 Summary: *The Duke returns; Isabella and Mariana publicly accuse Angelo. The Duke's disguise is revealed, and he shows mercy to Angelo, after Mariana and Isabella plead for him. Angelo is to marry Mariana, Lucio is to marry Kate Keepdown and the Duke proposes to Isabella.*

The Duke enters, now in his true guise, accompanied by the court and citizens of Vienna. Angelo and Escalus welcome him back. Isabella appears and asks for justice. The Duke responds that Angelo will give her justice, thus appearing to support Angelo while testing his hypocrisy further. Angelo denies Isabella's claims and the Duke pretends not to believe her. Meanwhile Lucio's interruptions annoy the Duke. When Isabella tells her tale, she omits the bed-trick, in accordance with the Duke's earlier instructions. The Duke orders that Isabella be arrested and calls for Friar Lodowick (the Duke's alter ego) to be brought before him. Lucio slanders the friar, not realising he is actually speaking to the same person – just as he earlier slandered the Duke, not realising it was the Duke he was actually addressing (3.1).

Mariana appears and refers to Angelo as her husband, revealing that she took Isabella's place in the bed-trick. Angelo admits they were previously engaged but claims he broke off the engagement because of the lack of dowry, adding an additional insult in slandering Mariana's reputation. Angelo loses his patience and says the two women's claims have been orchestrated by a more powerful figure behind the scenes.

The Duke leaves and re-enters as Friar Lodowick, denouncing Angelo. Escalus, alarmed at this public slander, orders that the friar be arrested and tortured. Lucio argues with the friar and pulls back his hood, revealing the Duke's disguise. Angelo immediately confesses his guilt and asks to be sentenced to death. He admits he was contracted to Mariana and the Duke orders that they be married immediately. The Duke still does not ease Isabella's mind with the knowledge that Claudio is alive. He orders the execution of Angelo but Mariana begs for his life, persuading Isabella to join her in entreating the Duke for mercy.

The Duke then reveals that Claudio is still alive, using the same moment to pardon Claudio and ask for Isabella's hand in marriage. He also pardons Angelo and Barnardine. At first it does not appear he will pardon Lucio, ordering that he be whipped and hanged after marrying the woman he wronged. However, the Duke relents, showing Lucio mercy too, although he must still marry.

Strikingly, there is no speech for Isabella to respond to the marriage proposal or the news that Claudio is alive. This is left for directors and actors to interpret.

Key point

Throughout the play we have seen Escalus act with moderation and fairness; yet, when the disguised Duke slanders Angelo publicly, Escalus appears to act in an extreme way; the friar is to be arrested and tortured. The severity with which Escalus acts reflects the seriousness with which early modern rulers viewed acts of public disobedience. Such actions were not considered to be ordinary crimes but a type of treason. People were not free to speak their mind, and publicly accusing a ruler or senior court official would have been extremely dangerous. This highlights the risk that Isabella and Mariana take in making their public claims.

Key vocabulary

Forerunning more requital (5.1.8): preceding further reward

Bonds (5.1.9): obligations

Characters (5.1.12): letters

Vail your regard (5.1.22): cast your gaze downwards

Conjure (5.1.53): entreat

Refelled (5.1.109): refused

Concupiscible (5.1.113): hotly desirous

Fond (5.1.121): foolish

Suborned (5.1.122): bribed to make false accusations

Punk (5.1.198): prostitute

Member (5.1.258): person

Cucullus non facit monachum (5.1.286): a hood does not make a monk (Latin)

Go darkly (5.1.302): question her cunningly

Light (5.1.303): promiscuous

Touse (5.1.334): pull violently

Giglots (5.1.370): harlots

Definitive (5.1.459): determined

Apt remission (5.1.539): ready forgiveness

Trick (5.1.546): custom

Executed (5.1.562): (wishes) fulfilled

Gratulate (5.1.570): pleasing

Q What is the Duke's punishment for Lucio?

Q A key aspect of the final scene is Isabella's silence. We do not know how Shakespeare intended her to respond. If you were directing the play, how would you instruct the actor playing Isabella and why?

CHARACTERS & RELATIONSHIPS

In the medieval theatre that predated Shakespeare, characters had less depth and were generally either embodiments of abstract ideas, such as vice, or figures known to the audience from biblical stories or historical tales. They fulfilled certain roles and functions in a play, making it less important to provide detail on the characters, since they were subservient to the overall structure of the play.

Shakespeare is credited with being among the first playwrights to provide a greater interiority to his characters. By 'interiority', critics mean that he gives us more information about what the characters think and how they feel about events, allowing audiences to construct a psychological profile for the characters. This depth is not provided uniformly across the characters; we learn more about some characters than others. There is also often complexity to Shakespeare's characters that helps us respond to them as plausible people. Very few of Shakespeare's characters can be reduced to a simple stereotype; there are often flaws in his heroes and elements of virtue in his villains. *Measure for Measure* presents a range of complex and interesting characters from all levels of society.

Isabella

Key quotes

'... she hath prosperous art
When she will play with reason and discourse,
And well she can persuade.' (1.3.70–2)

'I speak not as desiring more,
But rather wishing a more strict restraint
Upon the sisterhood, the votarists of Saint Clare.' (1.5.3–5)

Isabella is an extremely pious and chaste woman. When we first meet her, about to enter the order of Saint Clare, she appears disappointed at the level of restraint the nunnery represents; she would prefer greater strictures. This excessive nature in Isabella paradoxically aligns her with

Angelo, who is also presented as being excessive in his strict austerity. It is Isabella's extreme virtue that appeals to Angelo and inflames his desire.

At the core of Isabella's personal identity is her virginity. She wishes to live as a nun, which will involve taking a strict vow of chastity. Thus she is faced with a dire choice when Angelo attempts to blackmail her, insisting that she sleep with him as payment to release Claudio. To be true to her brother means betraying her core value.

Isabella's extreme piety results in her seeming quite heartless at some points. Furious at Claudio for asking her to save him, she says that 'I'll pray a thousand prayers for thy death, / No word to save thee' (3.1.159–60). Her excessive desire to remain virtuous at all costs results in a violent vehemence directed at Claudio. Nevertheless, in the final scene, when she is asked to choose between retribution or mercy towards Angelo, she chooses mercy, thus providing a model for the Duke.

Isabella's brother Claudio alerts us to another important quality of hers, when he tells Lucio that she is skilled in rhetoric, the art of persuasion. We see this in 2.2 when Isabella presents a range of compelling arguments in her appeal to Angelo to save Claudio's life. Given that Isabella has a powerful voice, it appears contrary that she is about to embark on a life as a nun in which her voice will be silenced. The strength of Isabella's voice also renders the ending of the play particularly problematic. Isabella must experience a rush of emotions at the end, learning her brother is alive, and at the same time receiving the Duke's proposal. Yet she is silenced by the playtext. Directors and actors must thus interpret her response in light of her character, and convey it through body language.

Key point

The depiction of Isabella's character raises questions about extreme human behaviour, relevant to the play's examination of temperance. She is not only chaste but seeks an excessively restrained life. For most people, chastity is not a feature of normal human behaviour and is contrary to a flourishing society, so does the play critique this type of choice? On the other hand, given the constraints on women in early modern society, particularly the often negative aspects of marriage – which included the risks of childbirth and a lack of power in the home – Isabella's stance could be viewed as a reasonable response to her society, and a claim for personal autonomy.

Angelo
Key quotes

'... A man of stricture and firm abstinence ...' (1.4.13)

'... a man whose blood
Is very snow-broth: one who never feels
The wanton stings and motions of the sense,
But doth rebate and blunt his natural edge
With profits of the mind, study and fast.' (1.5.61–5)

We first hear of Angelo in the words of the Duke. He describes him as 'precise' (1.4.53), meaning Puritan, and almost superhuman: he 'scarce confesses / That his blood flows, or that his appetite / Is more to bread than stone' (1.4.54–6). In 1.5, Lucio also describes Angelo as a person who is not subject to the ordinary human passions and appetites.

The descriptions of Angelo at the beginning of the play create a parallel with Isabella. She, too, appears beyond ordinary human impulses, and the mention of Angelo's practice of 'study and fast' (1.5.65) links him with the restrictions Isabella will undertake as a nun. Both figures seek to remove themselves from ordinary physical life. Lucio wonders whether Angelo is in fact human, citing rumours that he was born of a 'sea-maid' (3.1.388), a mermaid, and that 'his urine is congealed ice' (3.1.390–1).

Escalus describes Angelo as 'so severe' in dispensing the law that he seems to be the personification of Justice itself (3.1.530–2). Applying the law in the early modern period usually resulted in harsh punishments so 'justice' was generally contrasted with 'mercy'. Escalus is not complimenting Angelo here but rather implying that he is too severe, as he is pure 'Justice' with no degree of mercy.

Despite the deceptive nature of Angelo's appearance, however, and his 'angelic' name, he turns out to be a hypocrite. Contrary to his cultivated persona of control over his physical appetites, once he encounters Isabella he is driven by desire. Despite having arrested Claudio on the charge of premarital sex, Angelo attempts to force Isabella to sleep with him, in exchange for her brother's life. When, in 2.1, Escalus asks Angelo to put himself in Claudio's shoes, Angelo claims: ''Tis one thing to be tempted, Escalus, / Another thing to fall' (2.1.18–19). Later in the play, when Angelo does succumb to temptation, these earlier words underline his hypocrisy.

When Angelo reflects on his desire for Isabella, he recognises the paradox that it is her virtue that has aroused him: 'From thee, even from thy virtue' (2.2.192). He acknowledges that she has not consciously tempted him, and is amazed that it is her goodness that has caused the feelings in him: 'Can it be / That modesty may more betray our sense / Than woman's lightness?' (2.2.198–200). There is a disturbing violence in his imagery: 'Shall we desire to raze the sanctuary / And pitch our evils there?' (2.2.201–2). He seemingly wants to destroy the innocence that she represents. This causes him to interrogate himself, as if he were internally divided: 'What dost thou? Or what art thou, Angelo? / Dost thou desire her foully for those things / That make her good?' (2.2.203–5). He also recognises his hypocrisy; what he has condemned in Claudio he now finds himself drawn to.

In the final scene, when Angelo is forced to confess his guilt, he immediately asks for a strict sentence: 'Immediate sentence then and sequent death / Is all the grace I beg' (5.1.398–9). This extremity is in keeping with his character, reflecting his lack of moderation in all things. The Duke is like-minded, and states that Angelo is to receive the same punishment that he gave to Claudio, 'measure still for measure' (5.1.441). It is the intervention of Mariana, and then Isabella, pleading for mercy that models for the Duke what a just ruler should do.

Key point

A key mystery in the play is the way Angelo becomes seized with desire for Isabella when he is by nature a strict moralist, and Isabella is particularly chaste and pious. It is this extreme chastity, in both of them, that paradoxically fuels his lust. He seems to recognise in her a characteristic of his own, an excessive desire for restraint from ordinary human impulses. It is this suppression, in conjunction with the appeal of Isabella's virtue, that leads to his violent behaviour, and disregard for her own feelings or the responsibility of his position.

The Duke

Key quotes

'The duke yet would have dark deeds darkly answered, he would never bring them to light.' (3.1.454–6)

'A gentleman of all temperance.' (3.1.515)

The Duke is an ambiguous and often dubious character in the play. His decision to step down from power, leaving Vienna in the hands of Angelo, can be criticised as inconsistent with his obligations as ruler. The repressive law that Angelo presides over was put in place by the Duke; at the same time, the flourishing brothels suggest he has not been effective in creating a healthy, functioning society.

The Duke claims that he does not like the public performance aspect of wielding power (1.1.72–3). His plan is to go in disguise as a friar, so he can spy on his city and observe how Angelo exercises power in Vienna. The use of disguise gives him a slightly sinister nature, expressed in Lucio's observation that the Duke 'would have dark deeds darkly answered' (3.1.455). The Duke's surveillance creates dangers for ordinary subjects; Lucio's slandering of his ruler almost costs him his life.

Several of the Duke's actions are questionable. He withholds from Isabella the information that Claudio is still alive, making her suffer, just so he can determine when she will receive comfort from him: 'But I will keep her ignorant of her good, / To make her heavenly comforts of despair, / When it is least expected' (4.3.111–13). The Duke thus appears manipulative, orchestrating events and controlling others like a theatre director.

Countering the more dubious aspects of the Duke's character are the comments of Escalus. The Duke, in disguise, asks Escalus his opinion. Escalus outlines the Duke's various positive qualities, describing him as 'One that, above all other strifes, contended especially to know himself' (3.1.510–11) and who rejoices 'to see another merry' (3.1.513). His observation that the Duke is a man of moderation (3.1.515) conflicts with Lucio's earlier slander. Whose opinion do we trust? Escalus appears as a man of balance and wisdom in the play so Shakespeare encourages us to trust his judgement, yet Lucio is also often accurate about the Duke.

Although the Duke acts in some ways that appear to be helpful to other characters, his actions in the final scene contribute to the problematic nature of the ending. He publicly declares his intention to propose to Isabella, timed to coincide with the revelation that Claudio is alive and is pardoned. This assertion of power makes it difficult, if not impossible, for Isabella to refuse him.

Key point

The Duke puts Angelo in charge because he wants to rectify his own laxity in enforcing the laws. Yet, once in disguise, he finds out how Angelo has abused his power. At the end of the play, the Duke purports to show no mercy to Angelo; it is Mariana and Isabella who persuade him to show mercy. Thus the Duke, likewise, must learn how to be a just ruler.

Claudio

Key quote

'Sweet sister, let me live.
What sin you do to save a brother's life,
Nature dispenses with the deed so far
That it becomes a virtue.' (3.1.145–8)

Although Claudio is engaged to Juliet through a lawful contract, he sees Angelo's punishment as a reflection of divine condemnation. Claudio doesn't question the rightness of Angelo's harsh judgement. Rather he acquiesces to it and chastises himself, describing his own natural sexual desire as something evil. He uses a simile to draw a parallel between rats swallowing poison and humans giving in to desire (1.3.14). The distasteful image demonstrates how Claudio has internalised Angelo's Puritan stance and perspective.

Claudio comes across as a very human and relatable figure. Audiences can identify both with his failings and his fears. Through his moving speech at 3.1.129–44, which vividly imagines what we experience after death, we share his vision and the fear he is experiencing. Although at first he is adamant that Isabella should not compromise her virtue, he quickly changes his position once he contemplates what death may entail. He attempts to persuade her that if she were to save his life, the act would not be a sin.

Key point

When Claudio first asks Lucio to send for Isabella, he not only observes that she is skilled in rhetoric but also notes that 'in her youth / There is a prone and speechless dialect, / Such as move men' (1.3.68–70). That is, he is relying on her physical beauty to have an effect on Angelo. That Claudio intends to use Isabella in this way is unsettling and creates a subtle parallel with references to 'bawds' and prostitution in the play. Does his desperate situation justify using her in this way?

Escalus

Key quotes

'Of government the properties to unfold
Would seem in me t'affect speech and discourse,
Since I am put to know that your own science
Exceeds, in that, the lists of all advice
My strength can give you.' (1.1.3–7)

'I have laboured for the poor gentleman to the extremest shore of my modesty, but my brother justice have I found so severe that he hath forced me to tell him he is indeed Justice.' (3.1.528–32)

Escalus in the first scene is described by the Duke as skilled in matters of government and there is a suggestion that, until now, Escalus was perhaps senior to Angelo (1.1.47–8). Escalus is moderate and wise in dispensing justice. His name evokes the idea of 'scales', the symbol of justice; this reflects his wisdom in matters of governance. He lets Pompey and Froth off with a warning when Elbow arrests them, only imprisoning Pompey after a second offence. That Escalus is less hasty to send offenders to prison contrasts starkly with Angelo's harsh approach. Similarly, Escalus attempts to help Claudio, though to no avail (3.1.528–32). Escalus is also fair-minded, giving a respectful view of the Duke when asked for his opinion (3.1.513). His views contrast starkly with Lucio's and, since other moments in the play demonstrate his good judgement, audiences are more likely to trust his opinion than Lucio's.

Key point

When Escalus is asked for his opinion of the Duke, he answers in a positive way. Is this his honest opinion or is it that Escalus, having more wisdom than Lucio, is more careful and wary of being too free with his speech? Individual productions of the play can choose how to interpret and perform this scene, presenting Escalus as either ignorant of the Duke's disguise and giving an honest opinion, or as guessing the truth and thus answering tactfully.

Lucio

Key quote

'That fellow is a fellow of much licence.' (3.1.482)

Lucio is a character who moves between the lower and upper worlds of society. He assists Claudio by bringing Isabella to plead with Angelo and encouraging her not to give up when, at first, she is unsuccessful. Lucio is free with his speech, which puts him at risk at several points in the play. For example, he slanders the Duke, unaware that the latter is in disguise. When Lucio claims that the Duke is sexually promiscuous, it appears to reflect Lucio's own nature. Lucio frequents the brothels and is well acquainted with characters such as Mistress Overdone and Pompey Bum. Furthermore, he is not particularly virtuous; he abandoned Kate Keepdown after she became pregnant. At the end of the play Lucio, having annoyed the Duke once again with his interruptions during the final scene, is lucky to escape with only the punishment of having to marry his former mistress.

Key point

Lucio's varying modes of speech reflect his role in moving between upper and lower sectors of society. For example, in 1.5 Lucio speaks in verse to Isabella, whereas in the earlier scene 1.2, when he is with the low characters, he speaks in prose. His mode of speech alters according to the circle he is in.

The minor characters

A range of other minor characters helps to create the world of the play. **Elbow** is a key figure of humour with his malapropisms. He is unable to communicate what his allegations are, and misunderstands what others say. **Barnardine** also provides comic relief. In contrast to the tension created over Claudio's death sentence, Barnardine apparently has no fear of death – he simply refuses to consent to being executed on any particular day because he is unprepared. Thus somehow he has managed to evade execution for years.

The names of the characters often convey information about them. **Mistress Overdone**'s name has a bawdy innuendo, implying that the brothel madam is worn out from years of working as a prostitute. The name '**Pompey Bum**' indicates the character's ridiculous pomposity and that he belongs to the base world of the brothels. The executioner's name '**Abhorson**' suggests 'abhorred', the loathed nature of his job, as well as 'whore's son'. Also note the comical names mentioned in Pompey's soliloquy in 4.3 that reflect their personalities or professions.

THEMES, IDEAS & VALUES

Power and surveillance

Key quotes

'O, it is excellent
To have a giant's strength, but it is tyrannous
To use it like a giant.' (2.2.130–2)

'He who the sword of heaven will bear
Should be as holy as severe ...' (3.1.538–9)

Across his oeuvre (body of work), Shakespeare explored the nature of power. Since England was a monarchy, with no political power residing in the ordinary people, subjects were particularly vulnerable to the way in which rulers exercised power. Theatre was an effective political medium for presenting alternatives. In *Measure for Measure* we see the different ways in which power can be used: the law can be applied harshly, as under Angelo's regime, or with moderation, as Escalus advocates.

A ruler was believed to be divinely appointed, God's representative on Earth. Since torture and capital punishment were common in the period, rulers often held the power of life or death over their subjects, rendering monarchs particularly god-like. The play depicts how power can be grossly abused (as in Angelo's actions towards Isabella) and how the state can intervene in the personal lives of its citizens (in the actions of the Duke). Related to the exercise of power is the idea of surveillance. The Duke is an ambiguous and slightly sinister character as he spies on and manipulates the various characters, disguising his true identity. In Shakespeare's time the state was particularly repressive and employed spies to report on activities perceived to be contrary to the monarch's interests.

Ironically for a character who spends his time spying on others, the Duke reflects on how rulers are subject to the gaze of the people, at the mercy of their slanders and fantasies (4.1.62–7). Earlier in the play the Duke claims that he does not enjoy public life and 'ever loved the life removed' (1.4.9). This refers to the traditional opposition between the active life, at the centre of human politics and business, and the contemplative life, the life of quiet study and simple living. Although the Duke claims he does not enjoy life in the public eye, this was the responsibility of a ruler.

In Shakespeare's plays the political state is often represented as a garden, and the monarch as a type of gardener. Shakespeare uses metaphors and similes to convey the condition of the political state. For example, the Duke observes to Friar Thomas that strict laws are necessary 'bits and curbs to headstrong weeds' (1.4.21): unless laws are enforced, weeds (vices) will overgrow the garden of the state. This image is used again at the end of Act 3 when the Duke condemns Angelo for 'weed[ing]' the Duke's vice of laxity in enforcing the laws yet letting Angelo's own vices 'grow' (3.1.547). The Duke thus condemns Angelo's hypocrisy.

Key point

To what extent should rulers pry into and meddle with the lives of their subjects? Shakespeare raises this question through the actions of the Duke, who embodies state interference and surveillance. The law prohibiting extramarital sex also raises this question: to what extent should political power intersect with religious and moral issues?

Justice and mercy

Key quotes

'… No ceremony that to great ones 'longs,
Not the king's crown, nor the deputed sword,
The marshal's truncheon, nor the judge's robe,
Become them with one half so good a grace
As mercy does.' (2.2.76–80)

'The very mercy of the law cries out
Most audible, even from his proper tongue,
'An Angelo for Claudio, death for death!'
Haste still pays haste, and leisure answers leisure,
Like doth quit like, and measure still for measure.' (5.1.437–41)

Bound up with questions on the exercise of power are the ideas of justice and mercy. How should people be judged? Escalus reflects on the often arbitrary nature of earthly punishment; some are punished for small faults while others escape unpunished (2.1.41–3). In Shakespeare's time, punishments were often harsh for what audiences now might consider minor offices. There was also no guarantee of justice for the ordinary person, as the system created significant challenges for those with a rudimentary education, and without money or powerful connections to advocate for them. Claudio is unable to plead eloquently in his defence, so seeks Isabella to argue for him, since she is skilled in rhetoric. Thus the ability to obtain justice appears to depend at least partially on one's skills in oratory.

A humorous take on the justice process appears in 2.1. Elbow has arrested Froth and Pompey, and attempts to convey his allegations to Angelo and Escalus. However, he does not have a full grasp of the necessary vocabulary and his speech is littered with malapropisms. For example, he uses 'benefactors' (2.1.54) when he means 'malefactors' and describes the accused as being 'void of all profanation' (2.1.58), comically saying the opposite of what he intends. He is unable to obtain justice, and Escalus observes wryly to him that the accused 'hath some offences in him that thou wouldst discover if thou couldst' (2.1.185–6).

The play is alert to the difficult challenge for rulers, in finding the balance between justice and mercy. As Escalus recognises, showing mercy can cause individuals to reoffend: 'Mercy is not itself that oft looks so, / Pardon is still the nurse of second woe' (2.1.282–3). Yet he laments the plight of Claudio. Escalus is a figure who represents moderation in administering justice. In 2.1, he deals with Pompey and Froth in a practical and reasonable way, letting them off with a warning to mend their ways. This contrasts with Angelo's harsh treatment of Claudio. When Isabella pleads for Claudio, she reminds Angelo that mercy is the greatest attribute of rulers, who should imitate God's mercy towards mankind:

> ... How would you be,
>
> If he, which is the top of judgement, should
>
> But judge you as you are? O, think on that,
>
> And mercy then will breathe within your lips
>
> Like man new made. (2.2.95–9)

Yet Angelo fails to adhere to this Christian spirit.

The title of the play emphasises the importance of equality and fairness. It refers to a biblical passage (Matthew 7:1–2) promising that those who judge will be judged equally. When Escalus advises Angelo to exercise caution in administering the law too harshly, Angelo claims: 'When I, that censure him, do so offend, / Let mine own judgement pattern out my death, / And nothing come in partial' (2.1.30–2). Angelo asks that he should also be judged strictly, if he ever offends. When in 5.1 Angelo is forced to confess his guilt, the Duke accordingly pronounces his sentence. Yet the Duke also seems to misunderstand the application of mercy in administering justice. He states that the 'very mercy of the law' (5.1.437) requires an equitable response of a 'death for death' (5.1.439) and he sentences Angelo accordingly. It is Mariana and, at her persuasion, Isabella, who teach the Duke what the proper response of a ruler should be – to exercise mercy.

Key point

An important binary in the play is the tension between justice and mercy. In Shakespeare's age Christianity was the dominant ideology and the two books that comprised the Bible, the Old Testament and the New Testament, were often conceived as representing this tension. The Old Testament is the story of God's law and His punishment of mankind for disobedience in Eden, resulting in the Fall and humanity becoming mortal. On the other hand, the New Testament presents the idea that, through Christ's sacrifice and God's mercy, humanity was redeemed. For rulers to show mercy was, in theory, to act like Christ.

Sexuality

Key quotes

'As those that feed grow full, as blossoming time
That from the seedness the bare fallow brings
To teeming foison, even so her plenteous womb
Expresseth his full tilth and husbandry.' (1.5.43–6)

'Why, what a ruthless thing is this in him, for the rebellion of a codpiece to take away the life of a man.' (3.1.394–5)

One of the central themes of the play is sexuality, and the audience is presented with two extremes of sexual behaviour. At one end of the spectrum is Isabella, with her strict vow of chastity, and Angelo (as he first appears), who enforces a punitive regime against premarital sex, as a result of which Claudio is imprisoned and sentenced to die. However at the other end of the spectrum is the group of lower-class characters who are associated with the brothels and pubs: the seedy underbelly of Viennese society. In this world sex is sold as a means of living.

Between the two extremes of sexual behaviour are Claudio and Juliet who, although engaged, suffer the consequences of a harsh enforcement of the law against premarital sex. Their sexuality, arising naturally from their love for each other, is considered reprehensible in the strict eyes of the law, equated with sexual offences such as prostitution or adultery. Lucio expresses the severity of this, noting that it is extreme and irrational to take away a man's life 'for the rebellion of a codpiece': that is, for natural human urges (3.1.394–5). Furthermore, Vienna's strict laws and Angelo's new policy of unforgiving enforcement would, Lucio observes, 'unpeople the province with continency' (3.1.452–3), meaning the population will decrease because of the restraints on sexuality.

While most people in modern society perceive sexuality as a perfectly natural biological function, in the early modern period sexuality was often seen as inherently sinful and only permissible within the bounds of marriage. The attitude to sexuality in Shakespeare's period was largely governed by Church doctrine. According to the Bible, humanity was essentially 'fallen'. Adam and Eve's transgression, in eating fruit from the forbidden tree of knowledge in the Garden of Eden, had resulted in the Fall of mankind, expulsion from Eden and mortality as punishment. Sexuality was generally seen as something to be ashamed of, and a sign of humanity's flawed nature. The misogynistic construction of women at the time generally held that they were particularly liable to seduce men and give in to sexual temptation. Contrary to this general assumption about women, in the play it is Angelo who gives in to desire and is thus revealed as a hypocrite.

Key point

Lucio describes Juliet's pregnancy using imagery of natural fruitfulness (1.5.43–6). Her state is in tune with the flourishing cycle of nature, the imagery suggests. Shakespeare's language thus invites us to question the legitimacy of the strict laws of Vienna that appear to run counter to the natural human impulses necessary for a flourishing state.

Moral dilemma

Key quote

'Better it were a brother died at once,
Than that a sister by redeeming him
Should die for ever.' (2.4.111–13)

Part of Shakespeare's education involved arguing for one side of a debate and then the other. He was thus trained in the ability to approach issues from multiple perspectives. This is a feature of many of his works, which present cogent arguments on different aspects of an issue, or play out an idea through multiple characters.

A key idea in *Measure for Measure* is the moral dilemma. Isabella is presented with a stark choice by Angelo: she can save her brother's life but only if she sacrifices her chastity, a core aspect of her identity. The duties that face her are both equally compelling: protecting a brother's life, or adhering to a serious religious vow of chastity. To save her brother she must not only commit an act illegal under Viennese law but also condemn her soul. For Isabella, as a pious person, the prospect of eternal punishment is a far greater threat than the earthly one.

When Isabella rejects the idea of saving her brother through trading her body, Angelo says to her: 'Were not you then as cruel as the sentence / That you have slandered so?' (2.4.114–15). That is, he attempts to convince her that since he has offered her some power to save Claudio, she bears joint responsibility if she chooses not to use it. However, Isabella is quick to argue that there is no comparison between 'lawful mercy' (2.4.117) and the 'foul redemption' (2.4.118) that he is proposing she can provide.

Key point

The moral dilemma is explored in detail in the confrontation between Isabella and Claudio in 3.1. Through their competing arguments we are persuaded first one way and then another. This reflects Shakespeare's grammar-school education. The students often had to argue for one proposition and then argue on the other side of the debate. Across Shakespeare's work he gives us insights on issues from multiple perspectives; this adds depth and complexity to his work.

Gender identity and roles

Key quotes

'DUKE: What, are you married?
MARIANA: No, my lord.
DUKE: Are you a maid?
MARIANA: No, my lord.
DUKE: A widow, then?
MARIANA: Neither, my lord.
DUKE: Why, you are nothing then: neither maid, widow, nor wife?
LUCIO: My lord, she may be a punk [prostitute], for many of them are neither maid, widow, nor wife.' (5.1.190–9)

'[The engagement] was broke off,
Partly for that her promised proportions
Came short of composition, but in chief
For that her reputation was disvalued
In levity.' (5.1.237–41)

In Shakespeare's time, unmarried women were commonly constructed in reductive binary terms, as either virgins or whores. Religious ideology placed a high value on chastity, and sexuality in a woman was only acceptable within marriage, where its purpose was for the creation of children. Women were seen as naturally inferior to men and were associated with the body, while men were considered naturally superior and associated with the mind. Males were seen as more rational, women as more emotional. Women were also seen as weaker, more likely to give in to sexual desire, and less trustworthy than men. When Angelo considers whether the fault of his own lust lies with Isabella, he is embodying a common attitude that blamed women for male desire. Shakespeare often questions common assumptions of the time. While Isabella adheres to her vow of chastity, it is Angelo who is depicted as giving in to his desire, thus challenging the accepted gender stereotypes.

There was a great power imbalance between men and women in the period. Isabella is subject to Angelo not only because he is a ruler but because he is male. Similarly, at the end of the play, Isabella is vulnerable to the Duke's public proposal of marriage, not only as a citizen subject to her ruler, but also as a woman with comparatively little power. Note the double meaning of the word 'licence' Isabella uses at 2.4.152 when Angelo is putting his sexual proposal to her. The word evokes both authority and licentiousness; she recognises that Angelo is abusing and tainting his authority through giving in to his desire.

Mariana is vulnerable because of the broken engagement, particularly once she has slept with Angelo in the bed-trick. If the Duke had not ordered the marriage of Mariana and Angelo at the end of the play, Mariana would have been considered 'spoilt', a 'fallen' woman with few options to support herself. The exchange between Mariana and the Duke in the final scene (5.1.190–9) emphasises the vulnerability of women who were neither married nor virgins. Note how Lucio assumes Mariana is therefore a prostitute ('punk'). Angelo also insults her publicly with a false claim that he broke off the engagement in part because of her reputation. The Duke purports to rectify Mariana's situation by forcing

Angelo to marry her, although given the evidence of his previous conduct, the audience may have some misgivings about how well he will act as a husband.

Key point

Women were considered to be property and marriage contracts were, in part, a financial transaction, with betrothals involving the payment of a dowry. Mariana's dowry, the money that would have been paid by her family to Angelo in exchange for the marriage, has been lost at sea, resulting in Angelo breaking off the engagement. Similarly, it is for want of a dowry that Claudio and Juliet have not yet married, leaving them vulnerable to breaking the law.

Mind, body and moderation

Key quotes

''Tis one thing to be tempted, Escalus,
Another thing to fall.' (2.1.18–19)

'... And now I give my sensual race the rein ...' (2.4.169)

'I am sorry, one so learnèd and so wise
As you, Lord Angelo, have still appeared,
Should slip so grossly, both in the heat of blood
And lack of tempered judgement afterward.' (5.1.510–13)

A significant idea in the play is the relationship between mind and body, relevant to the themes of governance and sexuality. The mind, the seat of rational thought, was supposed to control the body, the animal part of the human, which was subject to sensual impulses and desires. The ideal state was thought to be one of moderation, an idea originating with classical authors such as Aristotle. Humans were to strive for temperance in all things, the rational mind controlling the body.

When we are first introduced to Angelo in the play, he is described as someone who is not subject to the senses (1.5.61–5). He is able to strictly govern his body and its appetites and the Duke appoints him to see how he will govern Vienna. Yet in 2.4, Angelo appears to quickly succumb to his desire for Isabella. He claims 'We are all frail' (2.4.126), attempting to justify his proposed transgression by arguing for the power of physical impulses. He also asserts that 'women are frail too' (2.4.130), stating a common belief that women were more likely than men to give in to the body over the mind. Yet it is Angelo here who is presented as the morally weak figure. In the final scene, Escalus expresses his disgust at Angelo's lack of moderation (5.1.510–13).

The various forced marriages at the end of the play can also be considered in light of the theme of temperance since they curb various imbalances that the play identifies. Lucio's licentiousness, and irresponsibility towards Kate Keepdown, are rectified by marriage. Similarly Angelo's excesses – his initial suppression of the body's impulses and then his violent desire for Isabella – are moderated through marriage to Mariana, which also answers his former injustice towards her. The Duke's proposal of marriage to Isabella functions in a similar vein, to counter Isabella's chastity and desire for extreme restraint. Both chastity and licentiousness are pulled towards a central ideal of moderation.

Key point

Early moderns often thought of the mind as the seat of rationality, as the divine part of humanity, whereas the body, subject to the appetites and the senses, was the animal part. It was through the body that humanity was susceptible to the temptations of the Devil and sin. Moderation in all things was the ideal for which people were to aim.

Death

Key quotes

'To sue to live, I find I seek to die,
And, seeking death, find life. Let it come on.' (3.1.43–4)

'Death is a fearful thing …
Ay, but to die, and go we know not where,
To lie in cold obstruction and to rot,
This sensible warm motion to become
A kneaded clod; and the delighted spirit
To bathe in fiery floods or to reside
In thrilling region of thick-ribbèd ice,
To be imprisoned in the viewless winds,
And blown with restless violence round about
The pendent world: or to be worse than worst
Of those that lawless and incertain thought
Imagine howling – 'tis too horrible!
The weariest and most loathèd worldly life
That age, ache, penury and imprisonment
Can lay on nature is a paradise
To what we fear of death.' (3.1.127, 129–43)

Claudio is condemned to die and the Duke, as friar, attempts to placate him, and help him face the inevitable with resolution. Claudio is at first persuaded by the Duke's rhetoric that life is insubstantial and hardly worth living: he seems prepared to accept death. Yet once Isabella presents him with a slim chance of reprieve, Claudio expresses the full fear of death.

An alternative response to death is presented through Barnardine. He appears to care little whether he lives or dies; the Provost describes him as 'a man that apprehends death no more dreadfully but as a drunken sleep, careless, reckless, and fearless of what's past, present, or to come: insensible of mortality and desperately mortal' (4.2.150–3). Barnardine has a humorous disregard for death yet manages to constantly evade it by refusing to die on a particular day because he has been drinking or is otherwise unprepared. This creates a comic effect, providing light relief from the tension surrounding Claudio's sentence.

Key point

When Claudio articulates the natural human fear of death, his speech contains little certainty of the Christian narrative of life after death. This contrasts with Isabella's pious confidence that he will go to heaven. Claudio's language seems to imagine a no-man's-land of existence, between the mortal and spiritual. His vision departs from orthodox Christian ideology of the period.

Slander

Key quote

'No might nor greatness in mortality
Can censure 'scape. Back-wounding calumny
The whitest virtue strikes. What king so strong
Can tie the gall up in the sland'rous tongue?' (3.1.463–6)

Words are shown to be a powerful tool in the play. When they are used effectively they can persuade others to accept particular arguments. On the other hand, the inability to use words skilfully results in a failure to communicate and can impede access to justice, evidenced by Elbow's malapropisms. Words can also be a weapon, affecting reputation and social standing. In 5.1 Angelo slanders Mariana, attempting to tarnish her reputation in order to justify breaking off the engagement. At several points Lucio defames the Duke, who later reflects on the fact that the status of rulers cannot protect them from the effects of slander.

In 5.1, when Isabella publicly denounces Angelo, the Duke pretends not to believe her and has her arrested for slandering Angelo. In the early modern period citizens were not able to speak freely and publicly about their rulers. To do so could prompt accusations of treason and even lead to death. Lucio is lucky to escape serious punishment for his words, while Isabella takes a risk in accusing Angelo and is at the mercy of the Duke. His initial reaction (pretending to disbelieve her and having her arrested) seems particularly harsh to a modern audience, even though ultimately she is vindicated.

Key point

When the Duke reflects on the potent effect of slander in 3.1, he suggests that calumny (slander) can strike at 'the whitest virtue' (3.1.465). However, the play raises questions about the nature of the Duke. The audience may not believe everything that Lucio says, yet they may also be sceptical of the Duke's claims to 'whitest virtue', particularly as it is his disguise and intermeddling in the lives of his subjects that leads to him hearing the slanders of Lucio.

DIFFERENT INTERPRETATIONS

Different interpretations arise from different responses to a text. Over time, a text will evoke a wide range of responses from its readers, who may come from various social or cultural groups and live in very different places and historical periods. Responses by critics and reviewers can be published in newspapers, journals and books, both online and in print. They can also be expressed in discussions among readers in the media, classrooms, book groups and so on.

While there is no single correct reading or interpretation of a text, it is important to understand that an interpretation is more than a personal opinion – it is the justification of a point of view on the text. To present an interpretation of a text based on your point of view, you must use a logical argument and support it with relevant evidence from the text.

The critics' viewpoints

Literary criticism, often referred to as 'secondary sources', is writing about a text, the 'primary source'. Literary criticism analyses, comments on and offers a particular interpretation of the primary text. In writing about a text, literary critics are entering into a dialogue with other critics and so try to take into account the opinions of others. Since Shakespeare's work has been around for a long time, there is a substantial amount of critical material about his plays and poetry. This can be daunting for students. Whether you are required to research some literary criticism as part of your study of the play will depend on your level and the expectations of your teacher. If you are required to, keep in mind that it is not possible for anyone to read and understand everything that is relevant to the play. Try to select a few articles or book sections that discuss an area of interest to you. Reading literary criticism should be enjoyable and is intended to help you to order your thoughts and shape your own ideas about the play. It can also open your eyes to aspects of the play that you hadn't noticed.

As well as literary criticism, every stage production or film of a play will present a different interpretation of it. A particular production constitutes an interpretation because directors, script editors, cinematographers and others make choices: for example, to cut, add or rearrange lines and scenes. Choices are also made regarding casting, acting, directing, costumes, sets, props, music, sound and visual effects, all of which are aspects that allow varying interpretations of the play. Audiences will also bring their own experiences to the play and respond to it in subjective ways. Enhance your reading of criticism by viewing some film and television versions of *Measure for Measure*.

If you are new to Shakespeare it is useful to start with some background information about his life, historical period and why he has proved to be such an enduring writer. Some excellent places to start are Jonathan Bate's *Soul of the Age* (2008), his earlier work *The Genius of Shakespeare* (1997), Stephen Greenblatt's *Will in the World: How Shakespeare Became Shakespeare* (2004) and Peter Ackroyd's *Shakespeare: The Biography* (2005). Also very useful are *The Oxford Companion to Shakespeare* (2nd edn 2015), with plot summaries and valuable critical and stage histories for each play, and *The Shakespeare Encyclopedia* (2009), which includes a wealth of images from the early modern period and contemporary stills from stage and film productions. *The New Cambridge Companion to Shakespeare* (2010) is also an invaluable resource with essays on Shakespeare's life, what he read, his language, genres, aspects of gender and the theatre of the time.

In terms of approaching *Measure for Measure* from the perspective of genre, valuable insights can be found in Kenneth Muir and Stanley Wells' *Aspects of Shakespeare's 'Problem Plays'* (1982) and Richard Hillman's *William Shakespeare: The Problem Plays* (1993). Penny Gay's *The Cambridge Introduction to Shakespeare's Comedies* (2008) has a useful chapter on the 'problem' comedies, including *Measure for Measure*. An earlier study by RA Foakes (1971) provides a useful overview of the 'dark comedies'. Also see the article by Leonard Tennenhouse (1982), who argues that *Measure for Measure* needs to be read in the wider context of 'disguised ruler plays' of the early modern period.

Scholarly editions of the play also provide a valuable introduction and overview, considering themes, historical and production contexts and aspects of characterisation; comparing editions can illuminate different approaches taken by critics. These can provide a useful starting point for determining which aspects of the play you wish to research. Jonathan Bate and Eric Rasmussen in the RSC edition (2010) provide a concise overview of the play's key issues, as well as sections on performance history and Shakespeare's career in the theatre. Brian Gibbons provides a comprehensive introduction to the New Cambridge Shakespeare edition (2006). Also look at the excellent introductions to the Oxford University Press (2008) and Arden (2009) editions of the play, and the Oxford School Shakespeare edition (2013) aimed at secondary-school students.

In seeking an overview of the diverse issues that the play raises, two excellent starting places are Marjorie Garber's chapter on the play in her *Shakespeare After All* (2004), and Katharine Eisaman Maus' introduction to the play in the Norton Shakespeare (3rd edn 2015). Kate Chedgzoy's concise volume on *Measure for Measure* (2000) is a great resource for relevant contexts and issues raised by the play; it also provides some visual materials.

Once you have an overall sense of the issues the play raises you can turn to resources that focus on particular aspects. Here are some examples:

- Debora Kuller Shuger's study (2001) provides valuable insights and historical contexts for the ways in which politics intersect with theology in the play.

- MW Rowe (1998) looks at the theme of temperance in the play, placing it in the historical context of Aristotelian ethics.

- Marcia Riefer (1984) provides a feminist perspective, exploring the way in which Isabella appears to increasingly lose her power during the course of the play.

Also useful are studies with a performance focus:

- Carol Rutter interviews two actresses that played Isabella in
  Clamorous Voices: Shakespeare's Women Today (1989) in order to
  gain insights into how actors approach the character in performance.
- Also see HR Coursen's exploration of the BBC television production
  (1984).

If you are researching a particular issue and your library has access to
databases, use the *MLA International Bibliography* and the *Literature
Online* databases. These will allow you to enter search terms and find
scholarly articles on your topic.

When using the internet for research, aim for peer-reviewed sites.
An invaluable place to start for *Measure for Measure* is the Internet
Shakespeare Editions series. This includes useful contextual information
on the play and offers various tools to manipulate the text, such as
showing all the speeches of particular characters.

Two contrasting interpretations

Any text is open to contrasting, yet equally valid, interpretations. Here
are two different arguments on the ambiguous character of the Duke.

Interpretation 1: The Duke is an unfit ruler.

The Duke is presented as a suspect figure from the start. In the early
modern period, rulers were seen as divinely appointed; having been
chosen by God, monarchs could not simply delegate their power.
Across his work, Shakespeare explores the potential disasters that occur
in kingdoms when rulers are forced to leave, or voluntarily step down
from their positions. In *Measure for Measure*, the Duke's delegation
to Angelo creates an unjust state where an ordinary man like Claudio
faces execution for sleeping with his fiancée. Several other figures
involved in governmental roles express their concern at the harshness
of Angelo's position. 'Lord Angelo is severe' says the Justice (2.1.280),

and Escalus, seen to be moderate and just in his dealings with others, expresses sympathy for Claudio: 'but yet, poor Claudio! There is no remedy' (2.1.284). Similarly the Provost observes that Claudio 'hath but as offended in a dream! / All sects, all ages smack of this vice, and he / To die for't?' (2.2.5–7). Lucio expresses this in a more earthy way: 'Why, what a ruthless thing is this in him, for the rebellion of a codpiece to take away the life of a man' (3.1.394–5).

In disguising himself, spying on other characters and manipulating events, the Duke is presented as engaging in practices unbefitting a monarch. Lucio expresses this when he says that the Duke has 'usurp[ed] the beggary he was never born to' (3.1.375–6) – not realising it is the Duke, in disguise, to whom he is speaking. There is a risk that the Duke's interference and manipulation of events taints his dignity. For example, in arranging the bed-trick he becomes analogous to a bawd like Pompey himself, and arguably a hypocrite like Angelo. His manipulation of events also oversteps the mark when he – for his own ends – withholds the information from Isabella that Claudio has not been executed, leaving her to suffer longer than necessary. The Duke claims, in his speech on power at the end of Act 3, 'craft against vice I must apply' (3.1.554). Yet is this justified or dignified in a monarch?

Perhaps the Duke's most damning action is in the final scene when he proposes to Isabella. He claims to have behaved benevolently throughout, but the proposal undermines this. The Duke knows that Isabella wishes to live as a nun and yet proposes to her publicly, misusing his power to coerce her, so that it is difficult for her to refuse him. Her silence in response conveys the impossible position he places her in. In this final action, the Duke hypocritically appears little different from Angelo; in effect, he, too, demands Isabella as recompense for helping to save Claudio. This concluding image presents a bleak view of the future of justice in Vienna.

Interpretation 2: The Duke acts wisely and morally, in the best interests of his subjects.

The Duke can be seen, from an alternative perspective, in a positive light. He recognises that Vienna has become licentious and lawless because he has not enforced the laws. His state has become like a garden infested with weeds (1.4.21) and he takes positive steps to remedy this. He believes his deputy to be immune to the appetites of the body (1.4.54–6) and expects him to be strict in enforcing the law. Angelo thus becomes the Duke's instrument in returning Vienna to a lawful state.

As a monarch, the Duke has been unable to see what is truly occurring in his dukedom. Moreover, it would be very difficult for a ruler, in their own guise, to hear the direct truth from those around them. In disguise, however, the Duke is able to move among his people, and for the first time, obtain a more accurate viewpoint. He is able to observe his deputy in secret and test what Angelo is truly like, to 'see, / If power change purpose, what our seemers be' (1.4.56–7).

The Duke is also empathetic. After hearing of Isabella's plight, he resolves to help her while, at the same time, saving Claudio and rectifying the wrong that Angelo created in breaking off the engagement with Mariana. It is through the Duke's interventions that Isabella has a chance to save Claudio.

In assessing the Duke's character, we can weigh up the views of two different characters who express an opinion on him. On the one hand Lucio claims that the Duke is licentious ('had some feeling of the sport', 3.1.399) and is prone to drink (3.1.407). However there are doubts about Lucio's character; Mistress Overdone claims he has abandoned his pregnant mistress (3.1.477–9). On the other hand, Escalus states that the Duke is unselfish, 'rather rejoicing to see another merry than merry at anything which professed to make him rejoice' and 'a gentleman of all temperance' (3.1.513–15). Escalus is presented as a figure of moderation himself, dealing fairly with others, so his opinions should bear some weight in judging the Duke.

The Duke's proposal to Isabella, although at first seemingly against her wishes, in effect moderates her sterile chastity, which is presented as excessive and analogous to Angelo's initial character of strict puritanical austerity. Chastity is seen in as negative a light as excessive licentiousness. As Lucio recognises, excessive sexual restraint will 'unpeople the province' (3.1.452); sexual reproduction is necessary for the health of the society. What Vienna needs for a flourishing future, the play suggests, is the median position of moderation through marriage. Angelo and Mariana's marriage rectifies the earlier injustice, as does Lucio's forced marriage to his mistress. Claudio and Juliet's union is finally vindicated. The Duke and Isabella's marriage completes the theme of comic harmony at the end of the play: Isabella will provide a just and virtuous influence on the Duke, auguring a positive future for Vienna's government.

QUESTIONS & ANSWERS

This section focuses on your own analytical writing on the text, and gives you strategies for producing high-quality responses in your coursework and exam essays.

Essay writing – an overview

An essay on a literary work is a formal and serious piece of writing that presents your point of view on the text, usually in response to a given topic. Your 'point of view' in an essay is your interpretation of the meaning of the text's language, structure, characters, situations and events, supported by detailed analysis of textual evidence.

Analyse – don't summarise

In your essays it is important to avoid simply summarising what happens in a text.

- A **summary** is a description or paraphrase (retelling in different words) of the characters and events. For example: 'Macbeth has a horrifying vision of a dagger dripping with blood before he goes to murder King Duncan.'

- An **analysis** is an explanation of the real meaning or significance that lies 'beneath' the text's words (and images, for a film). For example: 'Macbeth's vision of a bloody dagger shows how deeply uneasy he is about the violent act he is contemplating, and conveys his sense that supernatural forces are impelling him to act.'

A limited amount of summary is sometimes necessary to let your reader know which part of the text you wish to discuss. However, always keep this to a minimum and follow it immediately with your analysis of what this part of the text is really telling us.

Plan your essay

Carefully plan your essay so that you have a clear idea of what you are going to say. The plan ensures that your ideas flow logically, that your argument remains consistent and that you stay on the topic. An essay plan should be a list of **brief dot points** covering no more than half a page.

- Include your central argument or main contention – a concise statement (usually in a single sentence) of your overall response to the topic. See 'Analysing a Sample Topic' for guidelines on how to formulate a main contention.

- Write three or four dot points for each paragraph, indicating the main idea and evidence/examples from the text. Note that in your essay you will need to *expand* on these points and *analyse* the evidence.

Structure your essay

An essay is a complete, self-contained piece of writing. It has a clear beginning (the introduction), middle (several body paragraphs) and end (the last paragraph or conclusion). It must also have a central argument that runs throughout, linking each paragraph to form a coherent whole. See examples of introductions and conclusions in the 'Analysing a Sample Topic' and 'Sample Answer' sections.

The introduction establishes your overall response to the topic. It includes your main contention and outlines the main evidence you will refer to in the course of the essay. Write your introduction *after* you have done a plan and *before* you write the rest of the essay.

The body paragraphs argue your case – they present evidence from the text and explain how this evidence supports your argument. Each body paragraph needs:

- a strong **topic sentence** (usually the first sentence) that states the main point being made in the paragraph

- **evidence** from the text, including some brief quotations

- **analysis** of the textual evidence, with explanation of its significance and how it supports your argument

- **links back to the topic** in one or more statements, usually towards the end of the paragraph.

Connect the body paragraphs so that your discussion flows smoothly. Use some linking words and phrases such as 'similarly' and 'on the other hand', though don't start every paragraph like this. Another strategy is to use a significant word from the last sentence of one paragraph in the first sentence of the next.

Use key terms from the topic – or synonyms for them – throughout, so the relevance of your discussion to the topic is always clear.

The conclusion ties everything together and finishes the essay. It includes strong statements that emphasise your central argument and provide a clear response to the topic.

Avoid simply restating the points made earlier in the essay – this will end on a very flat note and imply that you have run out of ideas and vocabulary. The conclusion should be a logical extension of what you have written, not just a repetition or summary of it. Writing an effective conclusion can be a challenge. Try using these tips:

- Start by linking back to the final sentence of the second-last paragraph – this helps your writing to flow, rather than leaping back to your main contention straight away.

- Use synonyms and expressions with equivalent meanings to vary your vocabulary. This allows you to reinforce your line of argument without being repetitive.

- When planning your essay, think of one or two broad statements or observations about the text's wider meaning. These should be related to the topic and your overall argument. Keep them for the conclusion, since they will give you something 'new' to say but still follow logically from your discussion. The introduction will be focused on the topic, but the conclusion can present a wider view of the text.

Essay topics

1   *Measure for Measure* is commonly described as a problem comedy.
    To what extent do you agree?

2   Choose two characters from the play and analyse the relationship
    between them. Discuss their traits and values.

3   The central moral dilemma of the play is whether Isabella should
    sacrifice her chastity to save her brother. How does the play present
    the arguments on both sides of the question?

4   *Measure for Measure* explores the exercise of power and how it
    can be used or misused. Analyse with reference to two or three
    characters.

5   *Measure for Measure* presents different attitudes to sexuality.
    Discuss, taking into account relevant historical contexts.

6   How does Shakespeare use imagery and figurative language to
    present the characters and ideas in *Measure for Measure*?

7   *Measure for Measure* presents common early modern attitudes
    towards women. Discuss with reference to two or three female
    characters.

8   Throughout *Measure for Measure* characters use rhetoric
    (persuasive language) to convince others of their arguments and
    points of view. Discuss with reference to two or three characters.

9   Although at first the Duke seems to have good intentions, by
    the end of the play the audience sees him as manipulative and
    untrustworthy. Discuss.

10 The ending of the play is unsatisfactory, leaving important issues
    unresolved. To what extent do you agree?

Vocabulary for writing on *Measure for Measure*

Act: major division in a play; in *Measure for Measure* there are five acts.

Blank verse: plain verse with no rhyming words at the end of the lines.

Dramatic irony: when the audience knows something that a character does not.

Early modern: the period 1500–1800 CE (common era).

Elizabethan: refers to the period during which Elizabeth I was on the throne (1558–1603). Plays written after her death in 1603, when James I became king, fall into the Jacobean period.

Foreshadowing: an idea, event or imagery within a literary or dramatic work that anticipates and indicates an event that will occur later in the narrative.

Genre: a category of literary or dramatic work with a set of conventions (rules) about the characteristics of that type of work. Examples are comedy, tragedy, history and tragicomedy.

Historical context: aspects of the society and culture of the period and the place in which a text was produced that may be relevant in reading and understanding the play. This could include events, attitudes, other texts, behaviours, objects, beliefs and values.

Iambic pentameter: a line of verse totalling ten syllables, with the stresses (beats) falling on every second syllable (*iambic*) and with five stresses to a line (*pentameter*).

Malapropism: use of an incorrect word in place of a word with a similar sound, usually with humorous effect.

Metaphor: word or phrase used to describe something else by way of direct comparison. The word in Greek originally meant 'carrying from one place to another'. For example, when the Duke says 'We have strict statutes and most biting laws, / The needful bits and curbs to headstrong weeds' (1.4.20–1), he uses weeds as a metaphor for vices.

Personification: figure of speech in which an abstract idea, inanimate object or animal is given human characteristics.

Prose: speech or written language that is not patterned, appearing like ordinary sentences in conversation. The word comes from the Latin word *prosa,* meaning 'straightforward discourse'. You will recognise it in the play when the lines of dialogue continue to the edge of the page.

Renaissance: in relation to English literature, the period from the late sixteenth century up until 1660. Shakespeare was writing in the English Renaissance period.

Rhyming couplet: two lines of verse, the last words of which rhyme. For example: 'I'll tell him yet of Angelo's request, / And fit his mind to death, for his soul's rest' (2.4.195–6).

Scene: a subdivision of an act in a play. It also describes the visual appearance of the space in which the action is located. The word 'scene' derives from a Greek word for the tent or booth behind the stage, in which actors would get changed. Eventually the outside of the structure was decorated to fit in with the drama, leading to the idea of 'scenery'. (Note, however, very little stage scenery and very few props were used in original Shakespearean theatre.)

Simile: similar to a metaphor but using the words 'as' or 'like'. For example, the Duke describes the laws that have been unenforced as 'like an o'ergrown lion in a cave / That goes not out to prey' (1.4.23–4).

Soliloquy: a dramatic speech spoken by a single character, usually when alone on stage.

Stage direction: a note in the text of a play that tells actors what to do. These are generally minimal in Elizabethan and Jacobean playtexts.

Verse: metrical writing. The word 'metre' comes from the Greek word for 'measure' and refers to a pattern of stressed and unstressed syllables. You can often identify it in the play when you see that a character's lines don't continue to the edge of the page. Verse lines are structured and shaped into particular patterns. In Shakespeare's plays the verse is in iambic pentameter and often uses rhyme. (The word 'verse' can also refer to a stanza, which is a paragraph in a poem, and to poetry in general.)

Analysing a sample topic

Before starting on an essay, carefully consider the implications of the topic. What is the question asking of you? What assumptions does it make? What key aspects of the text is it inviting you to address? Are there are any literary terms in the question that you need to check the meaning of?

Once you have established what the question is asking of you, draft a preliminary thesis statement (main contention). What do you think about this topic, based on your reading of the play? It can be useful to frame your thesis statement as a sentence beginning with, 'In this essay I will argue that …' Next, sketch out an essay plan of five sentences, comprising your thesis statement, three main points you will make (one sentence on each) and a concluding sentence that states how your evidence will support your argument. Alternatively, leave the conclusion until you have examined the evidence from the text thoroughly.

Once you have an essay plan in place, start collecting evidence for your essay by reading the text closely and gathering useful quotations. As you look at the evidence you may need to go back and modify your thesis statement and conclusion.

If the essay task requires you to consult secondary materials, you will also need to be reading scholarly, peer-reviewed articles and book chapters and incorporate some of this material into your essay. In this case, you will need to respond to the arguments of others. You may be citing them to support your argument, or you might want to disagree or qualify their argument. For example: 'As X argues, [outline their argument in your own words] and this is further supported by [cite your evidence from the text]'; 'Y states that: [insert quotation from Y]; however, I would qualify this assertion by adding that [add your thoughts on the text]';

'Z observes that [insert quotation or paraphrase], but in my view [outline your argument]'.

A useful resource for integrating secondary criticism in your work is Graff and Birkenstein's *They Say/I Say*. What you are doing is entering into a critical dialogue with other writers who have analysed the play. As writers we need to respect what others have said and respond to their arguments, while contributing our own perspectives and arguments.

Set out below is an expanded essay plan that provides ideas on how to approach a sample topic. Remember to include in your introduction key details such as the author, name of the text you are writing on and the date of publication. Also, clearly set out what your argument will be.

Topic

The play's central moral dilemma is whether Isabella should sacrifice her chastity to save her brother. How does the play present the arguments on both sides of the question?

Sample introduction

In *Measure for Measure* (1604) Shakespeare presents a difficult moral dilemma for the central character, Isabella. To save the life of her brother, Claudio, she must sleep with the corrupt Angelo. The decision is made particularly difficult for Isabella because she wishes to live as a chaste nun. Shakespeare does not suggest that there is a clearly 'right' or 'wrong' choice for Isabella to make; rather, the play presents arguments on both sides of the question. This essay will argue that Shakespeare's skill in language, rhetoric and debate enables his characters to forcefully persuade us of the merits of both cases.

Paragraph outline

Body paragraph 1: Isabella presents a forceful argument on why it is better for Claudio to die than for her to sacrifice her honour.

- It would be useful to start with the character of Isabella and why the choice she is presented with is so abhorrent to her. Find some representative quotations from the play to indicate her character.

- Next, outline for your reader some relevant historical contexts – for example, that people in the early modern period had a strong belief in the afterlife of the soul.

- Then look at key arguments Isabella makes in her speech to Claudio in 3.1.

Body paragraph 2: Claudio presents an equally forceful argument as to why Isabella should save his life.

- Here you can analyse Claudio's powerful arguments on why Isabella should save his life.

- Outline how, through Claudio, Shakespeare articulates the human fear of death. Use quotations to provide examples of Shakespeare's language.

- Conclude with some observations about Claudio's imagery being particularly striking because it doesn't appear to conform entirely with Christian ideology of the early modern period.

Body paragraph 3: Shakespeare's skill in language, rhetoric and debate create the power of the play's dilemma.

- It would be useful to discuss historical context. Consult some biographical reference material on Shakespeare to find out how, as a student, he was trained to argue for one side of a question and then another.

- Outline how this practice is reflected in the equally powerful arguments of both Isabella and Claudio.

- Present some examples of Shakespeare's use of language which you consider to be particularly effective in persuading audiences of one argument or another.

Sample conclusion

Measure for Measure presents a complex dilemma that invites an audience to consider what they would do in Isabella's shoes. Shakespeare uses rhetoric (persuasive language) firstly to articulate the magnitude of what Isabella is being asked to sacrifice, and then to express Claudio's equally anguished plea for his life, in language that powerfully expresses the natural human fear of death. Shakespeare's ability to engage his audience in this debate reflects his training in rhetoric and dialogic reasoning at school. Rather than presenting a didactic opinion on one or other of the moral alternatives, his ability to consider both sides of the argument allows a detailed exploration of the issues and contributes to the play's power.

SAMPLE ANSWER

***Measure for Measure* explores the exercise of power and how it can be used or misused. Analyse with reference to two or three characters.**

In the early modern period, ordinary people had little control over most aspects of their lives, so how rulers exercised power was of vital concern. In *Measure for Measure* (1604) Shakespeare explores the exercise of power through three key characters: Angelo, Escalus and the Duke. This essay argues that their different approaches enable Shakespeare to present a range of alternatives on the issue, and ultimately the play advocates for rulers to act with moderation, balancing the exercise of justice with mercy.

Angelo has a reputation for strictness and abstinence (1.3.13), associated with Puritanism in Shakespeare's period. At first it seems he is immune to ordinary human desires. The Duke states that Angelo 'scarce confesses / That his blood flows, or that his appetite / Is more to bread than stone' (1.4.54–6). To rectify his own laxity, the Duke appoints Angelo to apply the law strictly. Angelo orders that the brothels in the suburbs be closed down and arrests Claudio on a charge of fornication, sentencing him to death even though he only slept with his own fiancée, Juliet. Thus Angelo is too extreme in exercising his power; the sentence is out of proportion to the alleged offence. Furthermore, Angelo abuses his power when he attempts to bribe Isabella into sleeping with him. Later in the play Angelo recognises the magnitude of his hypocrisy and his abuse of power: 'A deflowered maid, / And by an eminent body that enforced / The law against it!' (4.4.22–4).

By comparison, Escalus is generally a model of moderation in his exercise of power, his name evoking the scales of justice. He is described by the Duke as wise in the administration of government (1.1.3–7). Escalus cautions Angelo that rulers should only 'cut a little' (2.1.6) and he shows discretion and mercy in dealing with offenders, although he is cognisant that showing mercy can result in individuals reoffending (2.1.282–3). It is only upon a repeat offence that Escalus sends Pompey to prison. Escalus also advocates for Claudio and, when unsuccessful, criticises Angelo for being the personification of Justice itself (3.1.530–2). Escalus presents a median position, between the extremes of Angelo's harshness and the Duke's laxity.

The Duke claims in Act 1 that he has been too lax in enforcing the law, and certainly Vienna appears to be a state of unhealthy extremes of both prostitution and sexual restraint. He also claims that he does not enjoy being subject to the public gaze (1.1.72–3) and has 'ever loved the life removed' (1.4.9). However, monarchs were thought to be divinely appointed, thus giving away his power is both irresponsible and contrary to God's will. Furthermore, he delegates his power to Angelo, who he knows to have wronged Mariana, rather than to the wise Escalus. The Duke is also manipulative in using his own power behind the scenes when he stays in Vienna in disguise to observe and test how Angelo acts in power (1.4.56–7). Although the Duke attempts to rectify Angelo's harsh actions by working to assist Claudio, Isabella and Mariana, his methods are questionable. Through arranging the bed-trick he is analogous to a bawd in a brothel. He also delays telling Isabella that Claudio is alive, and at first publicly discredits her story. He thus misuses his power, stage-managing events to suit his own ends; he combines the moment of revealing Claudio is alive with a public proposal to Isabella, using his power in a way that leaves Isabella with little choice in responding.

In sentencing Angelo, the Duke claims to exercise justice equitably by treating Angelo in the same way as Angelo treated Claudio, 'measure still for measure' (5.1.441). This resonates with the play's title and the idea of talion law, the retributive Old Testament justice of an eye for an eye. However Mariana and Isabella show the possibility of an alternative way to exercise power: through mercy. Earlier in the play Isabella had reflected on the importance of mercy:

> … How would you be,
> If he, which is the top of judgement, should
> But judge you as you are? O, think on that,
> And mercy then will breathe within your lips
> Like man new made. (2.2.95–9)

This alternative corresponds with the Christian ideology of the New Testament.

In *Measure for Measure* Shakespeare presents various approaches to the use of power by society's rulers. The Duke's initial laxity is contrasted with Angelo's harsh application of the law. Escalus presents a more balanced approach, an alternative of moderation in his dealings with the common people. The Duke's actions as a ruler are questionable in many respects, particularly his delegation of power, then secret surveillance of his subjects. When he passes judgement on Angelo in the final scene, the Duke believes that justice will be served by treating Angelo as he treated Claudio, measure for measure. However, Mariana and Isabella persuade him to exercise mercy. With Escalus as the Duke's advisor, and Isabella potentially as Duchess, how will Vienna be governed in the future? As a problem comedy, the play's ending leaves many questions open. Nevertheless, *Measure for Measure* ultimately argues for rulers to exercise moderation, and for justice to be tempered with mercy.

REFERENCES & READING

Text

Shakespeare, W 2010, *Measure for Measure*, Jonathan Bate & Eric Rasmussen (eds), The RSC Shakespeare, Macmillan, Houndmills, Basingstoke.

All quotations and most of the 'Key vocabulary' definitions have been drawn from this edition.

Further reading

Ackroyd, P 2005, *Shakespeare: The Biography*, Vintage, London.

Bate, J 1997, *The Genius of Shakespeare*, Picador, London.

—— 2008, *Soul of the Age*, Penguin, London.

Chedgzoy, K (ed.) 2000, *Measure for Measure*, Writers and Their Work, Northcote House Publishers, Horndon.

Coursen, HR 1984, 'Why *Measure for Measure*?', *Literature/Film Quarterly*, vol. 12, no. 1, pp.65–9.

De Grazia, M & Wells, S (eds) 2010, *The New Cambridge Companion to Shakespeare*, 2nd edn, Cambridge University Press, Cambridge.

Dobson, M, Wells, S, Sharpe, W & Sullivan, E (eds) 2015, *The Oxford Companion to Shakespeare*, 2nd edn, Oxford University Press, Oxford.

Driver, E, Forbes, S, Mapps, J & Trewby, M (eds) 2009, *The Shakespeare Encyclopedia*, Global Book Publishing, Sydney.

Foakes, RA 1971, *Shakespeare: The Dark Comedies to the Last Plays: From Satire to Celebration*, Routledge, London.

Garber, M 2004, *Shakespeare After All*, Anchor Books, New York.

Gay, P 2008, *The Cambridge Introduction to Shakespeare's Comedies*, Cambridge University Press, Cambridge.

Graff, G & Birkenstein, C 2010, *They Say / I Say: The Moves That Matter in Academic Writing*, 2nd edn, Norton, New York.

Greenblatt, S 2004, *Will in the World: How Shakespeare Became Shakespeare*, Norton, London.

Hillman, R 1993, *William Shakespeare: The Problem Plays*, Twayne Publishers, New York.

Kastan, DS (ed.) 1999, *A Companion to Shakespeare*, Blackwell, Oxford.

Kermode, F 2001, *Shakespeare's Language*, Penguin, London.

Muir, K & Wells, S (eds) 1982, *Aspects of Shakespeare's 'Problem Plays'*, Cambridge University Press, Cambridge.

Riefer, M 1984, '"Instruments of Some More Mightier Member": The Constriction of Female Power in *Measure for Measure*', *Shakespeare Quarterly*, vol. 35, pp.157–69.

Rowe, MW 1998, 'The Dissolution of Goodness: *Measure for Measure* and Classical Ethics', *International Journal of the Classical Tradition* vol. 5, no. 1, pp.20–46.

Rutter, CC 1989, *Clamorous Voices: Shakespeare's Women Today*, Routledge, New York.

Shuger, DK 2001, *Political Theologies in Shakespeare's England: The Sacred and the State in* Measure for Measure, Palgrave, New York.

Tennenhouse, L 1982, 'Representing Power: *Measure for Measure* in Its Time', *Genre: Forms of Discourse and Culture*, vol. 15, no. 2–3, pp.139–56.

Other editions

Shakespeare, W *Measure for Measure*, Internet Shakespeare Editions, Kristin Lucas and Herbert Weil (eds), University of Victoria, http://internetshakespeare.uvic.ca/Library/Texts/MM/

—— 2006, *Measure for Measure*, The New Cambridge Shakespeare, Cambridge University Press, Cambridge.

—— 2008, *Measure for Measure*, NR Bawcutt (ed.), Oxford University Press, Oxford.

—— 2009, *Measure for Measure*, The Arden Shakespeare Second Series, JW Lever (ed.), Bloomsbury, London.

—— 2013, *Measure for Measure*, Oxford School Shakespeare, Roma Gill (ed.), 2nd edn, Oxford University Press, Oxford.

—— 2015, *The Norton Shakespeare*, Walter Cohen, Stephen Greenblatt, Suzanne Gossett, Jean E Howard, Katherine Eisaman Maus and Gordon McMullan (eds), 3rd edn, Norton, New York.

Film and television versions

Measure for Measure 1979, dir. Desmond Davis, UK, BBC Shakespeare. Starring Tim Pigott-Smith and Kate Nelligan.

Measure for Measure 1994, dir. David Thacker, BBC. Starring Tom Wilkinson, Corin Redgrave, Juliet Aubrey and Henry Goodman.

Measure for Measure 2006, dir. Bob Komar, Lucky Strike Productions. Starring Josephine Rogers, Daniel Roberts and Simon Philips.

Websites

Shakespeare Birthplace Trust, http://www.shakespeare.org.uk/home.html

Blogging Shakespeare, http://bloggingshakespeare.com/

Shakespeare's Globe, http://www.shakespearesglobe.com/

Royal Shakespeare Company, http://www.rsc.org.uk/

Shakespeare in Education (British Shakespeare Association), http://shakespeareineducation.com/

Measure for Measure Internet Edition,
http://internetshakespeare.uvic.ca/Library/Texts/MM/

Australian and New Zealand Shakespeare Association (ANZSA),
http://www.anzsa.org/

Luminarium: Anthology of English Literature, http://www.luminarium.org/